Studies in
Writing & Rhetoric

IN 1980, THE CONFERENCE ON COLLEGE COMPOSITION AND COM-
munication perceived a need for providing publishing opportunities
for monographs that were too lengthy for publication in its journal
and too short for the typical publication of scholarly books by The
National Council of Teachers of English. A series called Studies in
Writing and Rhetoric was conceived, and a Publication Committee
established.

Monographs to be considered for publication may be specula-
tive, theoretical, historical, or analytical studies; research reports;
or other works contributing to a better understanding of writing,
including interdisciplinary studies or studies in disciplines related
to composing. The SWR series will exclude textbooks, unrevised
dissertations, book-length manuscripts, course syllabi, lesson plans,
and collections of previously published material.

Any teacher-writer interested in submitting a work for publication in this series should send either a prospectus and sample manuscript or a full manuscript to the Senior Editor for Publications,
NCTE, 1111 Kenyon Road, Urbana, IL 61801. Accompanied by
sample manuscript, a prospectus should contain a rationale, a definition of readership within the CCCC constituency, comparison
with related publications, an annotated table of contents, an esti-
mate of length in double-spaced 8½ x 11 sheets, and the date by
which full manuscript can be expected. Manuscripts should be in
the range of 100 to 170 typed manuscript pages.

The works that have been published in this series serve as models
for future SWR monographs.

Gender Influences: Reading Student Texts

Donnalee Rubin

<small>WITH A FOREWORD BY</small> NAN JOHNSON

Published for the Conference on College
Composition and Communication,
A Conference of the National Council
of Teachers of English

SOUTHERN ILLINOIS UNIVERSITY PRESS
Carbondale and Edwardsville

Production of works in this series has been partly funded by the Conference on College Composition and Communication of the National Council of Teachers of English

Copyright © 1993 by the National Council of Teachers of English

Printed in the United States of America
Edited by Patricia St. John-Doolin
Designed by Design for Publishing, Inc., Bob Nance
Production supervised by Natalia Nadraga

Library of Congress Cataloging-in-Publication Data

Rubin, Donnalee.
    Gender influences : reading student texts / Donnalee Rubin ; with a foreword by Nan Johnson.
        p.   cm. — (Studies in writing & rhetoric)
    Includes bibliographical references (p.   ).
    1. English language—Rhetoric—Study and teaching.   2. Sex differences in education.   3. College prose—Evaluation.
    I. Conference on College Composition and Communication (U.S.)
    II. Title.   III. Series.
PE1404.R83   1993
808'.042'0711—dc20   92-26313
ISBN 0-8093-1866-0   CIP

96 95 94 93   4 3 2 1

The paper used in this publication meets the minimum requirements of American National Standard for Information Sciences—Permanence of Paper for Printed Library Materials, ANSI Z39.48-1984. ∞

For
Burt

Contents

Tables

Foreword

Nan Johnson

IN THE LAST FIVE YEARS, THOSE OF US WHO TEACH WRITING
have become more and more concerned with how issues of gender
affect our pedagogies and our students. Many of us have let go of
what was probably always a naive notion—that it was ambitious
enough to focus on the displacement of current-traditional teaching methods in favor of process-oriented and collaborative teaching
strategies—and we are now in search of a professional agenda that
would somehow combine the pedagogical advances we have made
with a commitment to greater self-consciousness about how gender
textures the teaching situation and the lives and writing of our students. While we may have moved in the direction of such a commitment, few studies exist to help us define and shape teaching-
methods that would deal openly and effectively with the problems
that gender can create in our relationships with students.

In *Gender Influences: Reading Student Texts,* Donnalee Rubin
offers us this kind of help in her discussion of the effects of gender
on the way teachers read and evaluate student texts. Insisting that
gender is a "significant presence in the writing class that we need
to examine more closely" (1), Rubin argues that if we are to overcome the influence of gender stereotypes on our perceptions of
student writing, we must first recognize the implicit power of that
influence. Rubin examines the responses of thirty-one freshman
composition teachers to student writing and shows the negative effects of gender biases on assessment in particular cases that prove
that gender perceptions and expectations can influence assessment

decisions that seem neutral on the surface. Arguing that certain pedagogies are more likely to minimize gender bias than others, Rubin believes that teachers are more likely to overcome the influence of gender bias on their teaching if they adopt a process-based method and work intimately with their students through nondirective, supportive conferences. Rubin characterizes the conference/process-centered class as the type of environment in which *maternal teaching* can be cultivated. Rubin stresses that maternal can describe any teacher, male or female, who exhibits the nurturing and supportive qualities that the conference/process approach embodies. With a primary focus on the student's well being and development as a person and a writer, the maternal teacher is in a better position to overcome gender bias that could distort the interpretation of student texts. In order to increase our sensitivity to gender issues in assessment, Rubin recommends that teachers self-consciously engage in what she calls "responsive reading." Responsive reading "occurs when . . . we read with an eye toward providing the sorts of supportive feedback and dialectic exchange that will encourage our student writers to think for themselves and to revise effectively" (101). Rubin argues that when we commit to a responsive-reading pedagogy, we are more obliged to question our reactions to student writing along the lines of gender influence and to strive for self-conscious awareness of how our own inner male-female voices may distort our reading of student texts.

Combining an analysis of representative case studies of teachers struggling with gender bias with a review of relevant insights from feminist and reader-response theories, Rubin challenges us to become more aware of the inevitable challenge this issue presents. "The gap between what we feel as we read and what we are willing, or able, to admit needs to be carefully considered so that we can better understand the reasons behind our responses" (103). In this monograph, Rubin counters the claims of oppositional feminism that polarize male and female and argues instead that essentialist views of gender fail to recognize that the qualities of caring and nurturing that comprise thoughtful and self-conscious teaching can be achieved by any man or woman who places the integrity and individuality of the student above all considerations.

Acknowledgments

IT IS A PLEASURE TO ACKNOWLEDGE THE KINDNESS OF THOSE people who helped me write this text. Thanks to Tom Newkirk for his caring guidance and support; to Robert Connors for his generous advice; to Nan Johnson, whose piercing commentary impelled me to reshape the final chapter; to Patricia Sullivan, Jane Hansen, Sharon Oja, and Donald Murray for their valuable feedback; to Donald Graves and Patsy Schweikart, who helped me construct the initial study; to the teachers who gave so unselfishly of their time; to Michael Spooner for his gentle encouragement; and to Kenney Withers, Susan Wilson, Patty St. John-Doolin, and the rest of the staff at Southern Illinois University Press. Very special thanks are due Frank Devlin, whose patient reassurance and extraordinary critical reading challenged me to look at my work in new and surprising ways. I am most grateful for his wisdom and for his friendship. Finally, loving appreciation goes to my mother, Ruth; to my children, Gary, Dan, and Karen; and most of all to my husband, Burt, whose unwavering strength and devotion sustained me through some very difficult times. Without him, this text would not have been possible.

Gender Influences

1

Gender and Reading:
Theoretical Indications

THE QUESTION THAT UNDERPINS THIS PROJECT, IN A FRESH-
man writing class, what are the effects of gender on the way teachers
read and evaluate student texts? was prompted by my interest in
the work of several important theorists—David Bleich, Jonathan
Culler, and Norman N. Holland in reader-response criticism; and
Annette Kolodny, Patrocinio P. Schweikart, Jean E. Kennard, and
Hélène Cixous in feminist criticism, to name a few—who suggest
that our responses to literary texts are affected by whether we are
female or whether we are male. Although these writers do not address directly the question of the teacher as reader, their work raises
the possibility that teachers' responses to student texts might also
be filtered through a gender-based lens, making gender a significant
presence in the writing class that we need to examine more closely.
If, as these writers claim, male responses and female responses to
works of fiction and poetry differ, with men able to remain more
distanced from texts—and thus more objective—and women able
to join with the text and the characters in it in much more connected
ways, it seems logical that gender differences might also inform
the special occasion of teachers reading the essays that students
compose.

Moreover, if we extend to the teacher-student context what some
of these theorists say about the different ways gender can affect
reader response, more focused questions immediately arise. For example, if female teachers read male student texts in the same way
they read male-authored literature, do they become hostile, resist-

ing readers (as Fetterley [1978] and Schweikart [1986] suggest occurs), privileging only feminine concerns? Or do male teachers, unable to identify with feminine issues, devalue women's texts (as
Holland [1980] and Kolodny [1985] imply happens when males
read literature written by females), thus penalizing their female
students?

Although the scholarship I explore in this chapter suggests, albeit
indirectly, that these situations, and others equally as problematic,
could indeed occur, my own research indicates that the evaluative
stance teachers adopt can contradict these expectations, especially
in conference-based writing programs. In order to be effective responders to student texts, teachers of both sexes lean toward the
integrated male-female dimension so valued by Kennard (1986) and
Cixous (1984) and away from the irreconcilable gender oppositions
that Kolodny and Schweikart claim are necessary to preserve the
female identity. When writing teachers read student texts, the
qualities that are traditionally labeled masculine and feminine become important components of an effective response. When we as
teachers respond to our own students' writing, the feminine voice,
which has, in effect, been silenced in both women and men trained
as academic readers, intensifies, unifying the masculine and feminine in each of us rather than pushing us toward separate spheres.
Being evaluators strengthens our gender-based similarities and flat-
tens to a great extent our culturally inscribed gender differences.

The stimulus for my research evolved from the reading I have
done not only in composition theory but also in reader-response
criticism, cognitive psychology, and feminist criticism—fields with
significant relevance to our work as writing teachers. This searching
outside our own discipline is not new. James L. Kinneavy and
Robert Kline, Jr. (1976), for example, discuss how in the fifth cen-
tury, Proclus, trying to classify poetry by basic genres, was left with
a jumble of extras that he called "all those others left standing
around." The authors explain how composition theorists today are
left in a similar bind, for "when all of the important bibliographic
entries immediately relevant to composition have been detailed,
there still exist references which have (or should have) had considerable influence on composition theory and practice and which do
not fit neatly into the obvious perimeters of the discipline" (241).
They cite key studies in philosophy, speech analysis, and education,

while the 1987–88 *Bedford Bibliography for Teachers of Writing* notes strong ties between composition theory and history, linguistics, literary criticism, philosophy of language, literacy, psychology, and sociology. Thus, finding shared contexts between seemingly unrelated areas is not only appropriate for writing researchers, but desirable. Moreover, if people in other disciplines are studying how gender-based reading differences appear at the convergences of discrete fields, a further rationale is presented for examining this issue in the specific circumstance of teachers reading and evaluating student texts.

All of the theorists discussed in this chapter converge at one key point: either implicitly or explicitly, all raise the question of how gender can affect the way we perceive and respond to reality. What emerges from the works we shall examine is an interlocking set of oppositions, bound together by a common curiosity about how gender acts as a determining force, particularly when we read. All the theorists agree this basic question is important, but when we investigate the issue, we notice one key difference in defining these oppositions. In their examination of the question, the reader-response critics and the cognitive psychologists talk in terms of conventional male-female divisions. But the feminist critics move beyond this simple contrast, breaking into two distinct camps—those who see gender as a weapon or tool with which to protect hard-won territorial concerns and those who recognize the power of gender as a unifying force. For both feminist groups, reading texts becomes a metaphor for reading ourselves and the world around us, and awareness of gender influences as we read becomes an elaborate framework for literary as well as personal interpretation.

Before considering the various theories, we need to acknowledge that gender is an incredibly complex term. The concept of gender presumes a clear-cut distinction between male and female that in actuality is often blurred. Yet we accept this presumption easily. For many people the matter is simple: the terms *female* and *male* constitute definable realities, opposite poles of a continuum on which movement away from either end is judged abnormal. Gender, however, is far from simple. In a search for its elusive definition, Anne Constantinople (1973) examines information from major tests of masculinity-femininity but asks how we can measure accurately something that seems so difficult to circumscribe. *Something*, she writes, is being measured by all the M-F tests, but what that some-thing *is* is almost impossible to pin down. Alfred B. Heilbrun (1981) also tries to explain sex-role behavior and the expectations society places upon individuals to conform, but he too admits that a struggle exists to define and measure a subject matter so often vague with a methodology so imprecise.

In addition, Sally McConnell-Ginet (1987) points out the dangers inherent in trying to separate interlocked behaviors. "We cannot," she reminds us, "focus on sex in isolation from the other factors that shape our lives" (164). Sexual differences do not outweigh all other characteristics. We are unable to point to a particular action and say this happened because she is female or he did that because he is male. Gender works in tandem with too many other ingredients to yield helpful information on its own. Like other variables, such as race, intelligence, financial status, or age, it rarely operates alone; rather it interacts with many environmental and experiential ele-ments, producing cognitive and behavioral patterns that often bol-ster our stereotypes and expectations.

These patterns seem well established and clear. But problems arise when we try to apply these rules to everyone. Hester Eisen-stein and Alice Jardine (1987) feel that "gender is a learned or ac-quired fact of social life" and that " 'male' and 'female' qualities . . . [exist] potentially" in all (xvi). Stereotypical masculine and feminine traits can be listed, but no person is, of course, entirely female or entirely male. Our qualities are often shared or exchanged, and be-haviors become even more difficult to assess as they cross the boundaries of imaginary gender norms.

Cixous (1984) would concur. "All human beings," she feels,

> are originally bisexual . . . there is always, in every human being, a complex relationship . . . passive and active . . . exchanging, spending, and retaining . . . it does not depend on the anatomical sex, not on the role of man and of woman, but . . . it depends in fact on life's chance. . . . I do not believe in sexual opposition nor in a sexuality that would be strictly feminine or strictly masculine, since there are always traces of original bisexuality. (131–36)

Cixous refuses to acknowledge male-female relations in terms of the rigid bipolar constraints that surround most discourse about men and women. For her, masculine and feminine, rather than being sexual labels, are processes of perception determined by what Verena A. Conley (1984) calls the "mode of arrival": for men, "children happen from the outside. . . . To women, they arrive from the inside" (119), a difference that alters each gender's relation to the "other." Gender oppositions, then, become a play of differences instead of distinct contrasts.

Nancy J. Chodorow (1987) complicates the matter even further by asking whether gender is best understood at all by focusing on discrepancies between men and women. "The concept of difference," she explains, "assumes the existence of an essence of gender so that differences between men and women are seen to establish and define each gender as a unique and absolute category" (4). But, she continues, "gender differences . . . are socially and psychologically created and situated. . . . Differences and gender differences do not exist as things in themselves; they are created relationally. . . . We cannot understand difference apart from this relational construction" (4). Chodorow cautions that

> to speak of difference as a final, irreducible concept and to focus on gender differences as central is to reify them and to deny the reality of those *processes* which create the meaning and the significance of gender. To see men and women as qualitatively different kinds of people, rather than seeing gender as processual, reflexive, and constructed, is to reify and deny *relations* of gender, to see gender differences as permanent rather than as created and situated. (16)

But despite all these reservations, many researchers acknowledge that using gender as a window or lens through which to view ourselves can be useful, in that it illuminates certain attitudes and behaviors we otherwise might not see. In an earlier work, for example, Chodorow (1978) examines the various ways in which gender seems to influence us as we undertake our daily tasks. Men and women, she claims, hold very dissimilar perceptions of human experience. Women view the world in terms of relationships. Men, however, see themselves as separate entities; their reality is not predicated on the sense of connection that females share. Building on this, Carol Gilligan (1982) also invites us to consider how gender appears to determine our perceptions. In her research, she finds gender a persistent shaper of our identity and moral development, with women seeking more communal experiences, while men stand firmly alone. Undoubtedly, we need more standardized, specific guidelines. But even though researchers recognize the difficulty in defining gender, they at least agree on differences in terms of *biological* identity, using that as a springboard for theoretical discussion. In this study then, *gender*, along with the terms *male* and *female*, will refer simply to biological determination.

Gender and Reader-Response Theorists

Three reader-response critics particularly important to this study, Culler, Bleich, and Holland, raise—both implicitly and explicitly— the question of gender as a determining force when teachers read and evaluate student essays. As a whole, reader-response critics share the belief that a text is not a stable thing that holds meaning but a variable entity that changes with each reader. To understand and appreciate a work, we need to concentrate on the process each reader undergoes as he or she reads, rather than on the text. These three theorists, however, look past the process of reading, asking key questions about the psychological predispositions of the reader before the reading task is ever begun. Their work helps us consider how gender, with all its accompanying cognitive and emotional baggage, manipulates or determines how we will negotiate a text. (For a brief discussion of other reader-response theorists who raise, by implication, questions about teachers reading students' texts, see Appendix A.)

Culler (1982) asks about gender openly. He reasons that "if the experience of literature depends upon the qualities of a reading self, one can ask what difference it would make to the experience of literature and thus to the meaning of literature if this self were, for example, female rather than male. If the meaning of a work is the experience of a reader, what difference does it make if the reader is a woman?" (42). If, as Culler suggests, a "work has structure and meaning because it is read in a particular way" (102), we might infer that we interpret the same works differently not only according to our preconceptions, which may to some extent be determined by gender, but depending upon the context and purpose of the whole reading situation. In order to understand, we have to ask, "How does one reach this reading? What are the operations which lead from the text to this representation of understanding?" (103). Culler also notes the claim of many feminist critics that "women's experience . . . will lead them to value works differently from their male counterparts, who may regard the problems women characteristically encounter as of limited interest" (45). This observation presents interesting possibilities, for it causes us to speculate whether gender could shape teachers' ideas and attitudes toward students' work just as researchers claim it does when readers interact with literary texts. For example, we might wonder if male writing teachers value the kinds of experiences their female students choose to write about. But Culler's work implies that the reverse might also be true—that female teachers also may have difficulty recognizing virtues in their male students' essays. These questions are significant in their suggestion that as teachers, we may approach each student paper with preconceived notions about students that we need to be aware of.

Bleich (1986) confronts the issue from a slightly different angle, insisting that reading is the sum of our subjective response, and his work shows how part of this response is closely tied to gender. He has noticed striking gender-based differences when his students respond to literary texts. In a study, similar to Elizabeth A. Flynn's,[1] of the responses of four males and four females, including himself, he found that men read prose literature differently from women but that both sexes read lyric poetry in similar ways. "The salient parameter," he explains,

> was the perception of the "voice" in literature. Men and women both perceived a strong lyric voice in the poetry, usually seeing it as the author's voice, while in the narrative, men perceived a strong narrative voice, but women experienced the narrative as a "world," without a particularly strong sense that this world was narrated into existence. Perhaps another way of articulating the difference would be that women *enter* the world of the novel, take it as something "there" for that purpose; men *see* the novel as a result of someone's action and construe its meaning or logic in those terms. (239)

As teachers, these differences in perception might work against us. When we read student texts, we try to read with an objective eye, separating our personal selves from our professional selves during the evaluative process. But Bleich implies that, because of our gender perspectives, this separation is not possible, especially if our students' essays are in the narrative form. Bleich feels that when males and females read lyric poetry, little difference in gender perception exists, and he attributes the similarities to "adult language features traceable to the acquisition of gender identity in early childhood. . . . The biology of the child, combined with his or her psychological relationship with the parents, creates a psychosocial gender interest that may be detected in that person's language throughout the life cycle" (262). Thus, when men and women read lyric poetry, they perform the same "action of self-objectification" as the poet, who writes in the self-reflexive "I." The lyric trope "recalls the action of language acquisition which renders the child capable of objectifying self and other" (262). "All readers of lyric poetry," Bleich notes,

> by noticing the author, by expressing concern for this author, by wanting to know about him or her, are going through the process of "separating" themselves from the maternal voice of the singer. . . . We readers naturally focus on the poet's "voice" and catch that singleness of its source in much the same way that we define the singleness of the original maternal voice. . . . Since we are adults, however . . . we [find] a way to affirm that "this is the poet's voice" and "this is my reading voice." (263)

The narrative voice, however, recalls a third person, the "father," and because we develop our gender identities in relation to *both* our parents, we can assume logically that males and females achieve their identity patterns in different ways. Girls move toward the mother and hence toward the mother's language. Obviously, for men this gradual pull away from the mother that makes each individual a distinct "I" involves a more radical process, a more painful separation than women undergo. Upon achieving gender identity, men become more "other," more likely to need a strong sense of individuality that will protect that otherness in a way women do not need. Thus, women can enter and join a text naturally because their selves rest on some measure of relationship or togetherness men can never know, while men find distancing from the text more urgent.

Although, as Patricia Sullivan points out,[2] Bleich ignores the possibility of anything other than a traditional nuclear family, his research raises several intriguing questions for writing teachers. If this gender imprinting indeed has the power he claims, then it seems reasonable that male teachers may find it easier to read students' texts objectively, while female teachers may lean more naturally toward some sort of fusion with the text—and with the writer as well. And with a student's first-person narrative essay, the problem could become even more complex; while both genders may show equal concern for the author because of a shared memory of the maternal voice, as happened with Bleich's readers of lyric poetry, the evaluative stance teachers must take removes us one step further from performing that same action of "self-objectification," and we may not be able to meet the author on his or her own terms.

When we raise the issue of gender in connection with reading, we raise, Bleich says, "the issue of who is reading, and we are saying that the readers are in some generic sense biologically defined. We are then wondering if biological boundaries of people have an effect on an activity that seems to be unbound by biological constraints: both sexes learn to read under the same circumstances and with the same expectations of success" (234). "How far," he asks, "do generic biological differences reach into the mental functioning of each gender?" (234). As Bleich outlines the distinctive ways in which he finds his male students and his female students read poetry and literature, he allows that men and women have common interests "that are permanently tied to the biological fact that they are of different genders" (266). His remarks suggest the possibility that as we read student papers, we exhibit male-female differences, which, examined openly, might make visible unconscious—and thus unarticulated—hidden agendas.

These concerns are amplified implicitly by Holland's (1980) assertion that "text and self are very close to experience" and that "interpretation is a function of identity" (123). For him, the overarching principle of interpretation is that "identity recreates itself." He explains that "we interpret the text in such a way as to cast it in the terms of our characteristic ways of coping with the world . . . each of us will find in the literary work the kind of thing we characteristically wish for or fear the most . . . to respond, we need to be able to re-create from the literary work our characteristic strategies for dealing with those deep fears and wishes" (124). Readers, Holland writes, will react favorably to those elements in a text that imitate in the work what the readers hope for. We do not read critically, he contends, "by resisting personal and emotional tendencies . . . the trouble is, reading can never be impersonal or objective. Critical skills serve a total conception of the poem rooted in the reader's character, drawing on all kinds of values and experiences which grow from the same roots deep in [the reader]" (117).

As writing teachers, we might educe from Holland that if gender-based differences prevent us from finding even a portion of our identities or wishes or fears in student essays, we may not be able to respond or react as objectively as we think we do. Male patterns and strategies of reading may not be useful when we confront female texts, and vice versa. We might need to develop a new set of strategies that will allow us to recognize our identity in more flexible ways, or we may be unable to cope with the new kinds of experience the text offers.

Holland states that we can accept the literary work "only to the extent that [we] exactly recreate with it a verbal form of [our] particular system of adaptive strategies [we] keep between [ourselves] and the world" (125). For our purposes, his contention is too limiting. Surely, if only for the reason that none of us is ever completely female or male but that we share characteristics traditionally attributed to the opposite sex, we are able to empathize with those elements of our students' experiences that are not a part of our own. Holland places too much of the burden of interpretation on the reader and then does not give us enough credit for being able to assume that burden gracefully. Our sense of self is bound to our sense of ourselves as male or female, and there are indeed strong differences between the two. But there are also similarities that bridge those differences. As humans, we function in a social, not just in a physiological milieu, and we are capable of adapting to each new context. However, Holland does emphasize implicitly the need to recognize that our gender identities, to a larger extent than we may imagine, could influence our perceptions of our students and their work. If what we read, be it literature or student writing, ceases to be a formalistic set of variables and becomes an organic experience in our minds, then our personal styles and identities become critical factors in determining not only the meaning of the text but also our reactions to it. If, as men and women, we are unable to find pleasure in the text because it makes no concessions to subconscious, gender-linked experiences, might we then as teachers subconsciously penalize our students for not re-creating our identity themes?

Gender and Muted Group Theory

Cognitive psychology offers other strong avenues for exploring the effects of gender on teachers reading student texts. Mary Crawford and Roger Chaffin (1986) consider muted group theory, first discussed by Edwin Ardener and Shirley Ardener (1975), which proposes that in a society where groups of people live in uneven power structures, the dominant group controls language and norms for its use. Members of the muted group have trouble articulating their experience as there are no terms for it in the language of the dominant group. And when members of the muted group do attempt the dominant language, some element of meaning is inevitably lost. This potential for misunderstanding works both ways, for members of the dominant group may ignore or miscalculate the importance of what the muted group is trying to say. Crawford and Chaffin note that the "primacy and centrality of the gender schema should ensure differential encoding of experiences by women and men" (23–24). But the academic world, especially, demands that women "adapt to the idiom of the dominant group, men, and . . . read and write like men" (24).

I suggest that writing teachers trained this way might experience difficulty. Teachers try to read student papers objectively, but for female teachers, there is an extra element to the task, for they are expected to suppress their natural tendency to perceive the world differently because of their gender and to evaluate student papers according to the dominant—or male—language in which they have been trained. (Feminist critics have long realized that the literary canon is male dominated, and that as students, we are trained to read male-selected literature with an eye directed toward male-established criteria.) In a situation where for so long the masculine has been seen as the prevailing discourse, female components of discourse become either insignificant or invisible, silenced certainly by men, but often, in effect, by women themselves because of their need to compete or to survive. This gendered problem with expression could easily transfer from the speaking/writing aspect of communication to the listening/reading side, implying similar difficulties when female teachers read student writing.

Approached from the other direction, however, the question of voice and identity becomes just as problematic for the male. If we accept Cixous' premise of a primal bisexuality—the inclusion of both the masculine and the feminine in every human being—then cultural repression of the feminine restricts full expression for the male as well as for the female. Thus the historical system of power relations, which constrains us, might trouble males as it does females. Although I suspect the long-standing alignment of males with the universal might cause the suppression of their female side to be less painful, we have to wonder how this muting of the male feminine unconsciously bends innate tendencies when male writing teachers read their students' work. Elsewhere in this discussion, this question will prove critical.

Gender and Feminist Critics: Oppositional Perspectives

Feminist criticism extends the possibilities for answering these questions—for considering the effects of gender on the way teachers read and evaluate student texts—not only by maintaining that gender-based reading differences exist but also by suggesting various reading patterns we can anticipate. It is an important field for us to examine for several reasons. First, it is closely allied with reader-response criticism because, as Schweikart (1986) explains, it elaborates on the two central preoccupations of reader-response theory: "(1) Does the text manipulate the reader, or does the reader manipulate the text?" and "(2) What is 'in' the text?" (48). Feminist criticism also explores this subject-object relationship between reader and text, but for feminists, Schweikart insists, "gender—the gender inscribed in the text as well as the gender of the reader—is crucial" (48). Second, and perhaps more significant, is that until recently, reader-response critics have not dealt with the question of gender-based reading differences. Rather, writers such as Wolfgang Iser and Georges Poulet have been preoccupied with setting up theories of reading that, because they never consider gender at all, reflect—by default, as it were—chiefly masculine concerns.

These writers, all male, can only discuss readers from a limited perspective. They have not considered that many readers are women, and that if readers determine the meaning of texts, then women readers might structure their interpretations in ways that deviate from male responses. The male writers we have already discussed assume implicitly that women's reading patterns will adjust somehow to their masculine ideal. When they do notice gender distinctions, as do Bleich and Holland, they offer no specific paradigm by which women can authenticate their own experience. But what I find even more distressing is that to discuss men's abstract theories of how women might read is to validate in some way what can only be an androcentric and alienated view, one step removed from what actually occurs. To understand the female reading process, we need to confront the reality of feminist critical practice, free from the patriarchal limits that push us into dualistic thinking. We must heed, however, Kennard's (1986) admonition that the differences between women are as myriad as the differences between women and men, and that to search for a reading process that embraces all women would prove futile. Although there is no one female perspective, the following feminist critics do help us understand some of the ways in which women's reading processes differ from men's. It is important to note, however, that they do so by setting up the familiar male-female opposition, encouraging—at the very least—a distinctly separate feminine domain.

Judith Kegan Gardiner (1981) examines how women approach texts, noting that women readers

> instead of guessing at and corroborating a stable identity pattern in a text or author, as Holland does, . . . approach a text with the hypothesis that its female author is engaged in a process of testing and defining various aspects of identity chosen from many imaginative possibilities. That is, the woman writer uses her text . . . as part of a continuing process involving her own self-definition. . . . Often encouraged by the author's shifting persons and perspectives, the reader shifts her empathic identifications and her sense of immersion in and separation from the text as she reads. . . . The woman writer allies herself intimately with her female

reader through this identification. Together they explore what is public and what is private, what they reject and what they reflect. (187–88)

She claims that female experience and identity prohibit women from significantly connecting with male texts, and this assertion raises essential questions for writing teachers. For example, if females share this close bonding experience when they read and write, what happens in the freshman writing class when female teachers read female texts? Are the female students in some way privileged because they have access to a complex female identity process that males can never share? Are the male students disadvantaged because their thinking and writing patterns automatically preclude empathic identification by their female teachers? If we teachers hope to become more self-aware readers of student essays, these are questions we need to address.[3]

Kolodny (1985) voices similar concerns. She discusses how women (I am reminded here of women as the muted group) have been excluded as participating readers from male-centered texts. Considering the situations female and male readers find themselves in when they enter the world of a text foreign to themselves in terms of gender-related issues, she observes that

> if neither language use nor language acquisition are gender-neutral, [but are instead] imbued with our sex-inflected cultural values [and if] reading is a process of sorting out the structures of signification in any text, then male readers who find themselves outside of and unfamiliar with the symbolic systems that constitute female experience in women's writings, will necessarily dismiss those systems as undecipherable, meaningless, or trivial. (148)

The same could also be true in reversed situations, where females are trying to read male texts. When teachers come up against a paper so female or male oriented in subject, approach, or tone, does that color their reaction or evaluation? Will a female teacher, for example, have problems with a paper on football, or will a male teacher have trouble relating to an essay on the latest fashion scene? We cannot overlook the implications of these kinds of studies or questions for our own teaching situations.[4]

Kolodny presents a reading theory closely aligned with Holland's—

namely, that when we read, we are attracted by those elements in the text that evidence traces of our own identity themes. But for Holland's generic male reader, this process is mainly subconscious: as we read, he explains, we interact with the work, interpreting it in ways that replicate ourselves. We

> work out through the text our own characteristic patterns of desire and adaptation . . . making it part of our psychic economy and making ourselves part of the literary work . . . each of us will find in the literary work the kind of thing we characteristically wish or fear the most. . . . The individual can accept the literary work only to the extent he exactly recreates with it a verbal form of his particular pattern of defense mechanisms and, in a broader sense, the particular system of adaptive strategies that he keeps between himself and the world. (124–25)

We are not aware of this activity as it takes place; rather we find ourselves inexplicably drawn to texts that allow us to recognize and use bits of our own experience, and we dislike or find little comfort in texts incapable of duplicating our own reality. Holland uses a basic tenet of psychology: we move toward pleasure and away from pain. But Kolodny would argue with Holland on two counts. First, the process she describes is a deliberately conscious effort. Second, she would resist any movement toward making her self a part of the literary text. As a woman, she is unwilling to sacrifice the smallest segment of her identity or to give up any measure of control.

Kolodny's (1982) interpretive framework rests on questions, on an active searching for collisions between the text's world and her own. She posits that "in bringing different analytical methodologies to any text, different literary critics necessarily report different gleanings or discover different meanings, meanings which reflect not so much the *text qua text* but *the text as shaped by* the particular questions or analyses applied to it" (159). And the particular questions Kolodny employs emphasize a singularly feminine perspective. She approaches a text from two key reference points:

1. How do contemporary women's lives, women's concerns, or concerns about women constitute part of the historical context for this work?
2. What is the symbolic significance of gender in this text? (175)

Her reading, then, is ever aware of and ever shaped not only by her gender but also by her use of what C. Wright Mills (1959) terms the "sociological imagination," the ability to transcend one's ego and place oneself in time and space within a larger historical frame. As she deliberately seeks the significance of female presence in the text, she also investigates how apparent gender behaviors in the work either elucidate contemporary gender distinctions or cloud actual sex roles.

Kolodny's agenda precludes any melding with the text, nor does it allow the psychological exchange Holland perceives. For Kolodny, reading is never a solitary but a social and political activity, an obligation to find and confirm validations of the feminine, and she seeks these confirmations in the company of and on behalf of all women. Her reading process challenges male critical conventions that fail to incorporate feminist perceptions and values. If this is true for all women readers, we need to investigate whether female writing teachers disadvantage, however unknowingly, writing composed by their male students who, in all probability, pay little heed to feminine concerns.

Schweikart's philosophy resembles Kolodny's in that she recognizes the political dimensions inherent in any feminist reading paradigm. For her the feminist story

> will have *at least* two chapters: one concerned with feminist readings of male texts, and another with feminist readings of female texts. In addition, in this story, gender will have a prominent role as the locus of political struggle. The story will speak of the difference between men and women, of the way the experience and perspective of women have been systematically and fallaciously assimilated into the generic masculine, and of the need to correct this error. Finally, it will identify literature—the activities of reading and writing—as an important arena of political struggle, a crucial component of the project of interpreting the world in order to change it. (39)

Here praxis is the chief purpose of writing, of reading, and of critical activity. Feminist readers work at dismantling the barriers presented by male texts, male interpretive strategies, and male suppression of female considerations. Schweikart would agree with Kolodny that the community of feminine readers commands a certain allegiance and that any feminine reading necessitates involvement that moves beyond the individual. Schweikart describes reading as a dialectic having three moments, a process in which the female reader maintains control. The first moment, she explains, is "marked by the recognition of the necessary duality of subjects" (54), the realization by the reader that although the text has been written by someone else, the reader becomes responsible for making meaning, and an illusory doubling of the reader's subjectivity occurs. With the second moment comes the "realization that this duality is threatened by the author's absence" (54). The doubling now presents a problem, for

> the subjectivity roused to life by reading, while it may be attributed to the author, is nevertheless not a separate subjectivity but a projection of the subjectivity of the reader. How can the duality of subjects now be maintained in the absence of the author? In an actual conversation, the presence of another person preserves the duality . . . in a real conversation, the other person can interrupt, object . . . provide further explanations, change her mind, change the topic, or cut off conversation altogether. In reading, there are no comparable safeguards against the appropriation of the text by the reader . . . reading is necessarily subjective. (53)

The need to prevent *total* subjectivity calls for the third moment, where "the duality of subjects is referred to the duality of contexts. Reading becomes a mediation between the context of writings and the context of reading" (54). The reader now must remember his or her own experiences, contexts, and premises, without imposing these on the author or the text. Schweikart's model allows for some measure of negotiation, but her aim is similar to Kolodny's in that she veils each reading through questions about the larger attention the text affords women and their concerns.

Schweikart implies a curious situation for writing teachers, for we deal with texts where the author is *not* a projection of the reader's subjectivity but a very real presence whose subjectivity we must acknowledge. As respondents and evaluators, how do we keep from imposing our own "experiences, contexts, and premises" on the author or on the text, especially when part of our job is to share our expertise? And in a writing class, how do we hold the realization that "although the text has been written by someone else," we as readers are "responsible for making meaning," when assuming responsibility for making meaning is something we are trying to teach our students to do? If, however, Schweikart is correct that male texts present hostile barriers that women need to topple, we have to consider how gender influences the dialectic between women teachers-readers and male students-writers. As teachers, seeing how our own reading patterns correspond with the model she presents might be one useful way to explore this problem.

Gender and Feminist Critics: Unifying Perspectives

While Gardiner, Kolodny, and Schweikart suggest, however unintentionally, that a generic feminine exists, other feminist writers eschew traditional male-female oppositions and support a more connected perspective. Kennard reminds us of the multiple categories within the feminine perspective and urges an embracing of these pluralities. Working from a lesbian awareness, she adapts elements of Joseph Zinker's (1977) theory of Gestalt therapy to pose a model of "polar reading," in which the reader acknowledges herself as a mixture of conflicting characteristics. "These polarities are not fixed," she suggests, for

> on different occasions the opposite of lesbian emotions may be those of a heterosexual female, a homosexual male, or even a heterosexual male. In this way the concept of polarities incorporates any differences that, under specific circumstances, can be defined as each other's opposite. . . . One's inner reality consists of both those qualities in one's self that one finds acceptable and those that are unacceptable and therefore often hidden or denied. (68)

For a reader, Kennard claims, this recognition of polarities means a "leaning into" rather than the resisting of the text that Judith Fetterley advises. The example she offers is that of a lesbian reading a heterosexual male text:

> Rather than resist the text, the reader grasps one familiar or shared aspect of the male protagonist . . . she "leans into" the character, identifies

with him as fully as possible, in a sort of willing suspension of belief. She uses the strategies she was probably taught so well; she reads like a man, but with a new awareness. Rather than experiencing schizophrenia, she allows the polarities to coexist. She forces the concentration on the heterosexual until the lesbian in her is pulled forward to the surface of her consciousness. (70)

"Leaning into" a text and respecting one's contraries rewards the reader with a reinforced sense of self. As Flynn and Schweikart explain, "Polar reading calls for the full recognition and the heightened awareness of the other, and of those aspects of one's self that are normally projected on others. The reader deliberately allows polarities to coexist. To the extent that she conducts the process freely and consciously, the result will . . . be . . . a deepening of and a consolidation of her sense of self" (xv).

Kennard's model, like Schweikart's, assumes a dialectic relationship between reader and text. Perhaps even more important though is her careful insistence that no one reader be privileged through the silencing of any other. For writing teachers, this seems a more desirable, more flexible pattern, one that would allow us as readers to value equally the writing of both women and men. We need to investigate whether gender-based reading differences preclude this balance.

The French feminist Cixous offers a final—and perhaps, for this discussion, the most critical—perspective. In a gloss of her work, Conley (1984) explains that Cixous' enterprise is "to read and write texts in order to displace the operating concepts of femininity in major discourses governing (Western) society" (5). For Cixous, reading is "writing, in an endless movement of giving and receiving; each reading reinscribes something of a text; each reading reconstitutes the web it tries to decipher, but by adding another web. One must read in a text not only that which is visible and present but also the *nontext* of the text, the parentheses, the silences" (7–8). Her reading is not a static enterprise but a continuous motion between her self and the page. She wants to read "how, when, and where [she] hears that [her] reading relates [her] to the real way [she] wants to transform it" (16). In other words, much like the American feminists, she maintains control at all times. But she emphasizes that control is not the same as mastery.

Echoing Schweikart, Cixous bespeaks a reading that is "always double . . . the reader/writer is unbound at the crossing of the unconscious demands of the text and her own unconscious" (21). As a reader, she is never separated from the writer, her "other." Moreover, she is ever bound to the double consciousness within herself— with both the feminine and masculine components of her being. When she interacts with the text, "the play of masculine, feminine, same, and other intersect at the textual level. . . . Reading at this limit, the inscriber intersects with the inscribed . . . where the critical text is not separated from the primary text which it controls. Separation is no longer identical to itself, reversible into its opposite; it is traversed by its own difference. The female reader/writer is the limit and the transgression of that limit" (33).

As she reads, then, Cixous is never one but a multiplicity of selves. Reading is never a simple operation but a "gathering" or "harvest," a circular embracing of her interior others. Her questions, unlike Kolodny's and Schweikart's, reflect more than just feminine concerns, for Cixous' view of the female and male present in all beings accompanies a sensibility unwilling to separate us into polar camps. We swirl endlessly into each other, and her reading acknowledges that constant blending of sexual difference into more than just the possibility of simple reversals. Where Holland and Kolodny search the text for traces of their identity themes, rejecting those texts from which their selves are absent and claiming inability to understand or sympathize with those texts containing foreign perceptions, Cixous, like Kennard, encourages a generosity that rejoices in difference. Her reading process respects strangeness, otherness, for to do so, she avows,

> does not mean that I relegate him to incomprehensibility; on the contrary, I seek to catch the most of what is going to remain preciously incomprehensible for me and that I will in any case never understand, but that I like, that I can admit, that I can tolerate, because really there is always a mystery of the other. In general, when there is a mystery, one feels hostility. One wants to destroy, one wants to oppose it. That is where I think there is an enigmatic kernel of the other that must be absolutely preserved. (144)

Cixous is willing to move toward a state where sexual opposites coexist rather than cancel each other out, not toward an androgynous circumstance, but toward a process in which neither sexual ingredient is repressed. If gender does influence writing teachers as they read student texts, Cixous (and I find her closely aligned with Kennard in this almost utopian view) offers a model of reading that promises to cancel bipolar limitations.[5]

Although these feminist critics suggest reading patterns they see as exclusively feminine, we cannot assume that all women read like feminist critics or that men never approach texts with any of these strategies. Nor can we believe that men have distinctive reading patterns that women do not share. These models do, however, provide a way to begin looking at our reading processes, and they raise provocative questions about how gender might affect teachers' reading and evaluation of student texts. Later in this study, when we look at teachers reading student papers, we will consider whether any of these paradigms apply.

Conclusion

Robert Scholes (1985) reminds us that when we read, "our choices in 'making' meaning are in fact severely limited by the writer's previous choices of what marks to put on the page" (154). "Texts," he explains, "have a certain reality. A change in a letter or a mark of punctuation can force us to perceive them differently, read them differently, and interpret them differently" (161). In other words, he would disagree with some of the theorists we have considered who see making meaning as solely the reader's responsibility. His argument is well taken. At some point we have to use common sense. As writing teachers we cannot blame ourselves constantly for any breakdowns or weaknesses in the process of reading and evaluating student texts. But the dialogues we entertain with our students are so complicated, we need to encourage a self-awareness born of our desire to understand the extent to which we *are* responsible. As Culler maintains, "In attempting to make explicit what one does when reading . . . one gains considerably in self-awareness . . . to refuse to study one's modes of reading is to neglect a principal source of information" (116).

The remainder of this text reinforces this call toward self-awareness. In the next three chapters, I consider, within the parameters of the scholarship we have explored, the influence of gender on freshman writing teachers as they respond to student essays. In chapter 2, I examine the responses of thirty-one freshman composition teachers to student writing and indicate the differing evaluative criteria that gender issues affect when instructors read students' texts. For this study I asked the teachers to discuss, in writing and in taped interviews, their reactions to four freshman essays. Although few significant gender-based reading differences appear in the written responses, the taped responses indicate problems in reading work produced by the opposite sex, which closely parallel those gender differences found by reader-response theorists when readers engage literary texts. Clearly, though, adding an evaluative dimension to the reading experience often distorts reader-response theory to some extent, and these distortions suggest how gender stereotypes and expectations could influence our perceptions.

The student texts I gave these teachers, however, were not the products of their own students, a circumstance that raised the issue of context: Would teachers exhibit these gender-dependent behaviors in connection with their own students' writing? In chapter 3, I explore this by monitoring, through taped interviews, the evaluation procedures of a male and a female writing teacher throughout their respective summer courses. Although the overwhelming weight of evidence from the scholars I have mentioned, as well as my earlier study with the thirty-one writing teachers, suggested that gender might play a significant role, the results of this second project reveal that actual teaching contexts, especially if they are conference based, confound our expectations. In teachers' interactions with their own students, bipolar gender-based reading differences dissipate, moving toward the sorts of male-female integrations embraced by feminist critics such as Kennard and Cixous.

In chapter 4, I consider the implications of this study for teaching and suggest questions for further research. I also discuss a key issue that arises from my research—the importance of the relationship between theory and practice. I then explain why, as a growing discipline, composition needs to rethink its dependence on literary theory and look toward its own pedagogical practice as a source of *new* theory and as a grounding for its clearly separate identity. I conclude by proposing a set of guidelines for *responsive reading*. If gender in any way shapes teachers' responses to student texts, how does this translate to a reading pattern we can anticipate and use to give more effective responses to our students and their work?

2

Gender Patterns: Reading
Student Texts

GIVEN THE IMPLICATIONS OF THE RESEARCH WE EXAMINED IN chapter 1, we might reasonably assume that male and female writing teachers respond to student texts differently. Moreover, we might expect these gender-based reading differences to lead to overall differences in assessment. However, in this chapter I will discuss how the responses of thirty-one writing teachers, eleven male and twenty female, to four student essays generally contradict these expectations. Both in the areas they commented on and the assessments they made, male and female teachers tended to concur. It was primarily in the way they formulated their responses that the differences noticed in our previous discussion seem to emerge. In this chapter I will explore how the context of teachers reading and evaluating student writing minimizes gender-based variations both in assessment and in recurrent patterns of concern. Except in the case of one essay, which we will discuss in the section titled "Significant Differences: The 'Euthanasia' Essay," the written responses indicate that male and female teachers attend to similar elements in the text. But the oral responses will demonstrate that as teachers are moved further away from the context of the evaluative task the power of that context dwindles. When we spoke, some of these teachers exhibited the marked gender polarities so prevalent in other cultural milieus and so evident in reader-response and feminist research.

This chapter develops along three main strands: (1) describing responses of these teachers to the four essays; (2) examining whether these responses relate to gender in any way; and (3) considering if gender influences these teachers' responses in a manner that limits or prevents effective interpretations of students' work.

Research Procedures

In this chapter, I used written protocols and taped interviews. Written protocols are established tools for collecting information about how writers work. I. A. Richards (1929), while admitting that "the astonishing variety of human responses makes irksome any too systematic scheme for arranging these extracts" (11), demonstrated the rich material available to researchers willing to seek out patterns in student responses. James Squire's (1964) work with adolescents reading literature was another landmark use of protocols, while Thomas Newkirk (1984) showed the impact the technique could have in composition studies. In addition to these written responses, I followed Squire's lead in using nondirective interviewing, an accepted method of collecting data in both social science and psychology (see especially Cannell and Kahn 1953; Muehl 1961; Phillips 1966; Dean, Eichhorn, and Dean 1967; Schatzman and Strauss 1973).

The Teachers
The thirty-one instructors were drawn from writing programs at two New England area schools. One group taught a one-semester freshman writing class at a large state university. This staff included graduate teaching assistants, full-time lecturers, and full-time assistant and associate professors. The second faculty taught a two-semester composition course. These teachers, at a small state college, were assistant and associate professors. The subjects responded voluntarily to a memo I passed out to the two freshman writing staffs. None of the instructors knew what the study was about. I told both staffs only that I was working on a special project and that I needed their help. Although I would have liked an even number of males and females, twenty females and eleven males responded.

Collecting Responses
I began gathering the written responses during the fourth week of the spring semester. Teachers were given copies of the four stu-

dent papers and an instruction sheet that read: "Please read these essays and answer the following questions as completely as possible. 1. What is your general reaction/response to each essay? 2. What grade would you give each essay? 3. Why?" The average length of the responses to all four papers combined was 287 words, including marginal and end comments.

In addition, I conducted in-depth interviews with four female and four male teachers who volunteered to meet with me. My choices here were limited by rather busy teaching schedules, but based on the differences in the subjects' ages and teaching experience, I feel reasonably assured that I received a fair mixture of responses and attitudes.

The Student Essays

Of the four student essays I asked the teachers to respond to in writing, two were authored by males and two by females. I did not give the instructors this information. Two of the papers were on gender-neutral subjects, euthanasia and the drinking age, while the other two were deliberately chosen for their strong gender-dependent issues, male-female dating habits. I wanted not only to elicit a variety of responses but to see how or if topic choice affects gender-related perceptions.

The student essays (which are reproduced in full in Appendix B) are fairly typical freshman efforts. All were written by students in my conference-centered freshman English classes and represent the students' own choices of topic and form. All were revised an average of three times as a result of teacher-student conferences and peer critiques. The following brief excerpts will suggest the flavor and approach of each piece.

1. The author of the drinking age paper clearly wants to change the law. His argument begins:

> One of the most controversial issues between young adults and state leg-islators is the drinking age. The drinking age is a state law that governs when a person is legally able to buy and consume alcohol. In many states, such as New Hampshire and Massachusetts, and Maine, the minimum age to legally purchase and drink liquor is 20. This law, however, is ig-nored by many 18 and 19 year old people because they are treated as adults in every respect with the exception of drinking alcohol. Drinking

requires responsibility and decision making, yet many more responsibilities are placed on 18 and 19 year olds. Therefore, I feel the drinking age should be lowered to 18 years old.

2. The female author of the euthanasia paper argues that euthanasia should not be considered a crime. Midway through the essay, she asks the reader to join her in solving the problem. "Imagine yourself," she writes,

sixty or seventy years from now, suffering from an incurable disease. Providing Medicare still exists, it is inadequate to cover your medical expenses. You live your final months or years in agony and continual pain. The disease slowly consumes your whole body. The medicine helps relieve the pain somewhat, but mostly it just prolongs the process and the suffering.

3. "Tough Guys," which incidentally was written by the same woman who produced the piece on euthanasia, is a bitter denunciation of the men at fraternity parties. In this essay, the writer's fierceness betrays her unspoken pain.

Well, girls, the days of chivalry, knights in shining armor, respect, and roses have ended. That's right, we've drifted into a new era: the age of tough guys "who think that they can do as they please." This line from a popular tune suitably sums up the situation, and you don't need to look far to find numerous examples of these gorgeous romping, stomping female satisfying men. After all, they *are* everything a girl could ever want, right? Wrong.

4. "How to Be a Hit with the Girls" is one young man's effort to poke fun at the seduction efforts of his peers. Witness, for example, our lothario advising others how to get ready for the big evening:

The first of your problems is how to dress. This, however, is not a particularly difficult one to solve. Your main objective in dressing is to blow your date away with your great taste in clothing. This can be done quite simply starting with a pair of Haggar stretch slacks and a red silk Gucci shirt, unbuttoned half-way down to show anything that might be growing on your chest. Next, get a pair of shoes with an unpronounceable Italian name. Driving gloves are optional, but if you do use them, make sure that they don't clash with your rented Ferrari.

The Written Responses

In order to analyze the written responses, I used procedures similar to Squire, who followed Bernard Berelson's (1952) suggestions for content analysis, and to Newkirk. First, I parsed the statements in each written protocol by using Squire's technique of breaking down the protocols into the smallest segments that conveyed a complete thought. For example, in the following typical response

> "The Drinking Age": This seems to me a rather ordinary and poorly thought out paper. I can't follow the logic as the writer moves from paragraph to paragraph. Though the writer seems to have considered the topic, he doesn't seem to have pushed thought beyond the obvious. The topic itself seems particularly unimaginative—a last minute desperation topic. I'd give the student some credit for organizing the information somewhat coherently and for writing some clear sentences.

the last sentence in the response cited above would be parsed: I'd give the student some credit for organizing the information somewhat coherently (1) and for writing some clear sentences (2). As Newkirk points out, excessive parsing "will result in statements that are not informative enough to code; if parsing is too infrequent, statements will contain references to more than one criteria" (287).

Once I parsed all of the responses, I began to look for patterns that would indicate ways to categorize the segments. For example, in one statement, I noted that the first parsed segment dealt with topic, the second with logic, the third with topic, the fourth with focus, etc. In this way, seven main categories emerged. Table 2.1 gives us a breakdown of two instructors' responses to the paper on the drinking age.

Reading Instructor 1 across shows us all the comments this instructor made about the essay; the second entry gives us Instructor 2's remarks. Using this method, I was able to categorize all but thirteen of the 1,392 parsed segments. (These thirteen miscellaneous remarks—e.g., "Oh God, I feel so wishy-washy," or "I hope I'm doing this right"—did not seem to fit into any particular category and were not included in the chi-square tests or in the tables.)

Table 2.1. A Breakdown of Two Instructors' Written Responses to
"The Drinking Age" by Category

Topic	Strategy	Focus	Style	Subjective responses	Judgments about Writer	Revision
Instructor 1						
Same old tired argument. Would work well with 18 year olds.	Not very convincing. Argues by false comparison. Fails to account for other side. Does try to develop its points, but fails. Points poorly developed. Outline of paper shows through.	Student wanted to get thesis in proper place.	First paragraph awkward. Grammar, syntax, & spelling lapses.	The sexism in the third paragraph is annoying.	Student is idealistic.	
Instructor 2						
	After disastrous first paragraph, gets paper under control & proceeds logically to conclusion. Uses familiar arguments. Basically well organized. Summary closing paragraph.		Diction awkward. Mechanics incorrect.	It's hard not to get mad at this paper.	Writer oblivious to need for law.	Student could profit greatly from conference.

Although there was no direct check on the reliability of the parsing (someone else might parse the statements differently), an indirect check occurred when two independent raters, a male and a female writing teacher, classified the parsed responses. I gave each rater the same one-third of the parsed responses, which I selected at random, and a list of the seven categories I had found. After I explained each category, each rater, working alone, placed each parsed segment into a category.

When I compared their charts to mine, the male had agreed with my classifications 83 percent of the time, while the female agreed with me 79 percent of the time. If both raters disagreed with my category assignment, we discussed it until at least two of us gave the segment the same classification. Here I followed D. Muehl's guidelines for check-coding in order to ensure which category constituted the most appropriate classification for each response segment.

Like Newkirk, I discerned that the responses fell into text-based (e.g., "This essay is poorly organized") and reader-based (e.g., "I really hate this paper") categories, but there was also a third division that seemed to be teacher- or evaluation-based, which consisted almost entirely of references to revision (e.g., "This paper needs to be rethought," or "I'd like to talk with the student about revising this"). I suspect this occurred because all of the subjects were teachers asked to perform an evaluative task. Listed below are the seven broad categories that emerged.

Text-based Responses

1. TOPIC
   References to the topic or subject of the essay

2. STRATEGY
   References to logic, strength or weakness of argument, support of argument or generalizations, reasoning, development of ideas and/or details, organization, order, structure, approach, awareness of audience

3. FOCUS
   References to focus, main point, thesis, main idea of essay

4. STYLE
   References to language, word choice, diction, sentence structure, fragments, run-on sentences, grammar, spelling, or punctuation

Reader-based Responses

5. SUBJECTIVE RESPONSES
   Comments that reflected personal reactions (e.g., "interesting," "boring," "offensive," "funny," "This paper turns my
   stomach"); refusal to grade the essay on grounds of sexism or
   offensiveness to reader

6. JUDGMENTS ABOUT THE WRITER
   (e.g., "This writer is a sexist pig!"; "I don't like this writer";
   "This writer has no idea what he's talking about. He needs to
   grow up"; "This student just tossed this off without thought")

Teacher-based Responses

7. REVISION
   References to the need to revise, redo, rethink, or rewrite the
   essay

Results

Tables 2.2 through 2.5 indicate for each of the four student essays the number of responses by males and the number of responses
by females in each of the seven general categories. In performing
all computations, I followed methods described by Neal Weiss
(1982).

In each cell of the tables, the observed value is reported, as well
as the number expected (in parentheses). For example, in table 2.2
the data for "The Drinking Age" show that in the male responses, 8
alluded to topic, 28 to strategy, 39 to focus, and so forth. In the
female section, 14 responses referred to topic, 43 to strategy, 69 to
focus, and so forth. The table shows a total of 125 male responses
and 221 female responses, for a total of 346 responses. Each parsed
segment counted as one response.

At the .05 level of significance, a chi-square of greater than or

Table 2.2. Observed and Expected Number of Male and Female Responses to "The Drinking Age" by Category

	Topic	Strategy	Focus	Style	Subjective Responses	Judgments about Writer	Revision	Total
Male								
Frequency	8	28	39	20	20	7	3	125
(Expected)	(8)	(26)	(39)	(16)	(19)	(9)	(9)	
Female								
Frequency	14	43	69	21	23	32	19	221
(Expected)	(14)	(45)	(69)	(15)	(27)	(33)	(17)	
Total	22	71	108	41	43	39	22	346

Table 2.3. Observed and Expected Number of Male and Female Responses to "Euthanasia" by Category

	Topic	Strategy	Focus	Style	Subjective Responses	Judgments about Writer	Revision	Total
Male								
Frequency	6	34	30	19	17	9	1	116
(Expected)	(5)	(26)	(30)	(23)	(13)	(6)	(14)	
Female								
Frequency	10	48	65	54	25	9	45	256
(Expected)	(11)	(56)	(65)	(50)	(29)	(12)	(32)	
Total	16	82	95	73	42	18	46	372

Table 2.4. Observed and Expected Number of Male and Female Responses to "Tough Guys" by Category

	Topic	Strategy	Focus	Style	Subjective Responses	Judgments about Writer	Revision	Total
Male								
Frequency	1	30	14	24	24	16	7	116
(Expected)	(2)	(25)	(16)	(23)	(23)	(12)	(8)	
Female								
Frequency	4	41	31	40	61	18	14	209
(Expected)	(3)	(46)	(29)	(41)	(55)	(22)	(14)	
Total	5	71	45	64	85	34	21	325

Table 2.5. Observed and Expected Number of Male and Female Responses to "How to Be a Hit with the Girls" by Category

	Topic	Strategy	Focus	Style	Subjective Responses	Judgments about Writer	Revision	Total
Male								
Frequency	5	26	11	25	52	10	2	131
(Expected)	(4)	(23)	(12)	(22)	(55)	(9)	(6)	
Female								
Frequency	5	33	19	32	89	14	13	205
(Expected)	(6)	(36)	(18)	(35)	(86)	(15)	(9)	
Total	10	59	30	57	141	24	15	336

Table 2.6. Areas of Significant Difference in Male and Female
Response Patterns to "Euthanasia"

Gender	Strategy	Style	Subjective	Judgments	Revision
Male	29%	16%	15%	8%	.9%
Female	19%	21%	10%	4%	17%

equal to 12.59 was necessary to indicate a significant difference between the responses of males and the responses of females to each
paper. For "The Drinking Age," a chi-square of 8.99 was obtained,
indicating no significant differences between male and female responses. The tables for "Tough Guys," with a chi-square of 7, and
"How to Be a Hit with the Girls," with a chi-square of 4.98, also
indicate no significant difference between the responses of females
and the responses of males. However, a chi-square of 26.2 was obtained for "Euthanasia," indicating a significant difference between
the responses of males and the responses of females to this essay
in the categories of strategy, subjective responses, judgments about
the writer, and revision. Table 2.6 indicates the percentage of the
total number of responses in these categories to "Euthanasia" according to gender. For example, the first line shows that 29% of the
male responses referred to strategy, while the second line indicates
that only 19% of the female responses fell into this category. The
differences between these responses, as well as the meaning of the
findings of no significant differences, will be discussed further.

Discussion

Despite my expectations, no significant gender differences occurred in the written responses to three of the student essays. But
key differences did emerge in the responses to the essay on euthanasia as well as in the way males and females formulated their responses to all four texts. In this section, I will consider how the
context of the evaluative task influences these differences. I will
also examine the effects of the gender biases revealed in the oral
responses.

Table 2.7. Percentage of Male and Female Responses to Three
Categories of "The Drinking Age"

Gender	Topic	Strategy	Focus
Male	6.4	22.4	31.2
Female	6.3	19.5	31.2

No Significant Differences: Three Essays

No significant differences appeared between the responses of males and the responses of females to three of the student papers, "The Drinking Age," "Tough Guys," and "How to Be a Hit with the Girls." Ironically, though, this fact in itself seems to be significant, since based on the research in chapter 1, we would have expected these differences to occur. But the similarities in the recurring patterns of concerns of both genders as well as the parallels in the nature of the responses indicate that something *is* happening that bears examination.

I suggest that the evaluative task I gave the teachers is responsible. So strong is the power of this context that even in the somewhat artificial situation I placed them in, the teachers were pushed toward the same sorts of behaviors they would display toward their own students, and the gender differences we would expect in assessment were suppressed. When I asked the teachers to read the essays, I gave them three questions to answer: (1) What is your general response/reaction to each essay? (2) What grade would you give each essay? (3) Why? With the written responses, that second question, the request for a grade, shifted the task enough toward the context of an actual teaching situation to blur gender distinctions; even the simulation of an evaluative context is strong enough to inhibit those gender differences evident when men and women read in nonevaluative situations.

To illustrate, let us examine the three categories with the highest correlation of response for "The Drinking Age" paper—topic, strategy, and focus. In each of these categories, similar percentages of males and females responded in similar ways. In table 2.7, for example, we see that 6.4% of the males and 6.3% of the females commented on topic. Clearly, the males and females pay equal attention to certain elements in the text. But the responses also share striking similarities in substance. Note the parallels between genders in the following remarks:

Male Responses to Topic
—Not another one—six yawns and a groan.
—Seldom have I seen a good essay on this topic.
—It's a chestnut topic, one that's hardly ever covered well.

Female Responses to Topic
—The topic itself seems particularly unimaginative.
—Having read roughly 10,000 papers on this subject, I don't consider it an original topic.
—This is one tired subject, and I did *not* want to read about it.

Male Responses to Strategy
—The writer does a good job of developing the notion of responsibility, citing four or five examples of what he/she means and tying them back to the argument that drinking is a responsibility too, yet even a lesser one.
—It's well argued, energetically argued. The argument builds well towards its strength.
—The writer has taken care to marshal a decent argument and support the case for lowering the drinking age by pointing out apparent contradictions in the system.

Female Responses to Strategy
—The paper proceeds logically to present four reasons and ends with a concluding paragraph. . . . In short, the paper is dutifully organized.
—The paper does a good job with providing concrete examples for each argument presented.
—The examples are there and the support for his arguments are good, and the structure is very good, a nice build to the climax.

Male Responses to Focus
—It makes a clear assertion and stays faithful to the main point from beginning to end.
—The writer has wisely decided to focus on one thing only, and he maintains the focus well.
—Has a good clear central idea.

Female Responses to Focus
   —The writing is competent and sticks to one point.
   —This paper contains a thesis, stated clearly in the intro-
   duction.
   —Main focus clearly spelled out.

Although the percentages of responses for each gender were not as
closely aligned in the remaining categories, it is important to note
here that in substance, the responses were as equally parallel as
those above.

   With this paper, as with "Tough Guys" and "How to Be a Hit with
the Girls," the strength of the evaluative context was such that male-
female differences in assessment were not significant. The context
itself seemed to repress the sorts of gender influences reader-
response critics and feminist critics find within the framework of
readers encountering literary texts. But with the essay on euthanasia, other factors come into play that weaken the ability of the evaluative context to inhibit gender-based responses and allow marked
differences between genders to surface in areas of concern as well
as in the nature of the responses. In the next section, we will examine the reasons for this breakdown.

Significant Differences: The "Euthanasia" Essay
   Because this paper was the only one to elicit significant differences between male and female responses, we first need to consider
how this essay deviates enough from the other three to warrant
measurable variations. In the case of "Tough Guys" and "How to Be
a Hit with the Girls," the difference seems clear: the euthanasia
essay adopts a persuasive stance about a serious topic, contrasting
sharply with the light satire of "Hit" and the angry narrative of
"Tough Guys"—personal essays that neither in subject, form, nor
tone fall easily into the category of traditional academic discourse.
From the first lines of these papers—perhaps even from just the
titles—a reader expects a rather playful piece. A reader beginning
the euthanasia and drinking age essays, however, anticipates a more
conventional approach.

   But with the drinking age paper the contrasts become more problematic. This is also a persuasive essay on a fairly serious topic, with
the author trying hard to convince his audience of the correctness

of his stance. But here the similarity ends. The male author of the drinking age paper states his case aggressively, backing up his opinions with details and illustrations of his points. Although his argument weakens in places, his feeling that the eighteen-year-old limit is unfair is presented in strong declarative sentences that move forcefully through the pages until they reach their logical conclusion: it is only right that the law be changed. The writer confidently assumes that the reader, having been given the information, will, of course, agree.

The female author of the euthanasia paper, however, puts forth her convictions in a less assertive way. Her feeling is clear from the beginning: euthanasia should not be considered a crime. But she relies on questions rather than statements to build her case, inviting her readers to participate in a way that the male did not. She hopes that her audience, rather than being lectured into submission, will gradually come to share her view. At one point she asks:

> What if you were the parent of a child that was in an accident that destroyed his brain or paralyzed him? He is placed on a life support machine because he can no longer take care of his own biological functions. You visit him every day yet he does not, he can not recognize you. You watch him regress to a small shrunken figure. Imagine the anguish you'd feel being totally helpless. As a parent wouldn't you like to be able to make a decision, to help stop the needless suffering?

This questioning approach signals the key difference between the two papers: the mode of presentation.

Thomas J. Farrell (1979) would cite both persuasive pieces as typical of what he calls the "male" and "female" rhetorical modes. Drawing on the work of Sarah D'Eloia (1976), he explains that when men write, they present their arguments within a much more direct and formal structure than do women. Men's thinking appears "framed, contained, more preselected, and packaged" (910) than women's thinking, which seems "eidetic, methectic, open-ended, and generative" (910); and these different thinking patterns are reflected in different written forms. Thus, writing in the female mode presents ideas that seem "less processed and controlled . . . than in the male mode and hence comes closer to recreating the process of thinking as it normally occurs in real life, where thinking is as much a matter of unconscious as of conscious processes and certainly does not move in formal logical structures even when it relates to them or reflects them" (910).

Although Farrell sees the female mode as requiring a greater degree of control than the male mode (and thus, perhaps, being the more difficult of the two structures), he sees the male mode as the method taught in academia; thus it is not surprising, he reminds us, that "many women . . . write and speak in the male mode" (909). Writers skilled in the female mode can, he insists, "use the male mode of rhetoric quite effectively when they choose" (920). But when the female author of the euthanasia essay did not make this choice, presenting instead a persuasive piece in the nontraditional academic form Farrell sees as feminine, she may have provoked the discrepancies between the male and female responses. Whereas the other essays did not activate this particular trigger, here male-female modes provided a stimulus strong enough to supplant the power of the evaluative context; the violations of the readers' expectations subverted the context enough to allow significant gender differences to surface both in the recurrent patterns of male-female concerns and in the contrasting nature of the responses.

The revision category indicated the greatest difference between the number of male and female responses, with 17% of the female responses, as opposed to less than 1% of the male responses, indicating suggestions for revision. The women teachers saw possibilities in this essay that the men did not seem to support. For example, one woman wrote: "This essay really has potential. This could be a dandy paper if she tried this angle. I'd love to talk with her about revising." Another offered, "This really effective paper could benefit from some minor revision. We could probably straighten this out in conference." These remarks typify the general feeling among the female instructors that whatever weaknesses they saw could be worked on to produce a better paper. In contrast, only one man mentioned revision in connection with this essay, but his remark was far from positive: "Not even extensive revision would save this awful piece."

This sharp disagreement about the essay's potential might be explained by the muted group theory (Crawford and Chaffin; and Ardener and Ardener), which we discussed in chapter 1, as well as by Farrell's classification of male and female modes. For example, if men and women trained as academic readers have their feminine voices silenced and are taught to read in male-oriented ways, it seems logical that they would more greatly value academic discourse produced in the male mode. We might expect, then, that the questioning techniques in "Euthanasia" would not receive high praise from either group. However, men—with feminine qualities silenced both academically and socially—might be less apt to recognize potential in an essay written in the female mode than women, whose feminine tendencies are acceptable within social contexts and thus more near the surface of their consciousness, and who might see more easily the promise in such a piece and be more inclined to offer suggestions for revision.

The work of Farrell and of Crawford and Chaffin can explain the differences between male and female responses in the four other categories that displayed significant differences as well. For example, the males seemed more disturbed than the females about the logic or structure of the argument, with 29% of the male responses faulting the logic and 19% of the female responses indicating favorable reactions. Note the parallels in the following responses of four male instructors:

The rhetorical questions are weak, the argument disorganized.

Here the argument wanders every which way, circles back, never sorts out dominant issues.

I don't find this argument convincing. It blurs some important distinctions and resorts too often to an easy kind of emotionalism which isn't balanced by some careful argument.

The paper does not seem to follow an outline, and the points are not effectively organized.

These men share reservations about those elements of the essay that distinguish it as Farrell's female mode. A persuasive essay, they seem to assume, is not supposed to be constructed in this manner. But the female instructors seem to accept this feminine framework more easily. The remarks of three women instructors characterize the general female response:

The paper is developed, at least for me, beautifully. There is a sense of moving back and forth on the points that shows a command, a grasp of the material. There is a sense of handling multiple ideas as points in a sentence—for me, the mark of a good writer. . . . The argument is presented in a reasonable manner. . . . Movement in this paper is clear.

This student had a direction and followed it. Student moved from a general to a specific point with ease.

Her thesis was clear . . . she is really working at developing a cogent argument.

(Note in this last response that even though I provided no information about the author, this reader automatically assumes the writer is female, a phenomenon we will explore in Appendix C.)

These women teachers follow what Farrell calls feminine thought patterns in the essay more comfortably than do the men. When they have problems with logic, they do not dismiss the entire work. Witness the following women's responses:

I find myself reacting when the writer mentions technology. I think the writer could strengthen the argument by focusing more on the technology and its inevitable problems.

The paper seems intended as an argument stating reasons for the writer's belief. But the reasons are not clearly delineated. The paper is not particularly persuasive.

(After this comment, the second reader expresses a desire to talk with the author about revising the piece.) The women, on the whole, did not feel excluded by the female mode as did the men, and they accommodated the flaws they did see by refusing to limit the text's possibilities for change. They made more frequent comments about style, 21% as opposed to 16% of the male responses, with most of the comments quite favorable. The males, on the other hand, found the style "trite," "hackneyed," and "too flowery." It is possible too that fewer male responses alluded to style because (1) in the grand scheme of things, style is not worth mentioning if something as important as logic is so weak; or (2) style is an element one works on during the revision stage, and the males found this essay too weak to save.

The remarks under the subjective responses and judgments about the writer categories indicate differences that seem to occur for reasons similar to those above. Fifteen percent of the male responses were subjective, as well as negative; for example,

My reaction as a reader = I'm bored.

I admit that I started to lose sympathy with the writer.

These responses contrast with the 10% of the female responses in this category, most of which were positive; for example,

Room for improvement but better than average work.

This paper is a delight to read.

The judgments about the writer also reflect the tendency toward male rejection and female acceptance. Eight percent of the total male responses made some sort of negative assumption about the writer; for example,

This writer just tossed this off.

The writer didn't give this any careful thought.

But 4% of the total female responses in this category were positive; for example,

The writer spent a lot of time on this paper.

The writer really cares about this issue.

The discrepancies in these two categories suggest that, as in the other classifications, the men had more negative comments than the women because they did not value a piece of academic discourse presented in this form. If they consider the male mode more suitable for a college essay, they might find the essay as written unacceptable. While women can "adapt to the idiom of the dominant group . . . and read . . . like men" (Crawford and Chaffin 24), this accommodation does not appear to work both ways, and the written responses to the euthanasia essay indicate that the author of this paper may be subject to this academically and socially imposed limitation wherein male readers devalue female texts.

There is, however, a crucial point to keep in mind here. Although I placed the teachers within an evaluative context, they were still removed from the reality of their own teaching situations; the context here was only simulated. We cannot assume that within the framework of their own teaching situations the teachers would respond in similar ways. In interpreting the responses to this essay, I am not suggesting that male teachers respond in this manner to their own female students' texts. In fact, chapter 3 will confront precisely this point.

Formulating Responses: Gender-based Approaches

Although the essay on euthanasia was the only paper whose written responses indicated significant differences between the concerns of males and the concerns of females within the specific categories, distinctive variations occurred between the ways in which males and females formulated their responses for all four essays. For example, even though similar percentages of males and females might have referred to, say, topic, they did differ in how they shaped their responses to this aspect of the paper. When we examine these responses, we see strong parallels to those differences noticed by researchers who have studied the contrasts between male and female responses to literature. Bleich and Flynn, for instance, suggest that males find it easier to read objectively, while women naturally gravitate more toward an involved, closer relationship with the text. The teachers I worked with mirrored these reading behaviors.

For example, when I asked the instructors to respond in writing to the three basic questions—What is your general response/reaction to each paper? What grade would you give each paper? Why?—I gave no other instructions. I wanted each teacher to react instinctively in the most natural or comfortable way. Seventy percent of the women wrote directly on the papers, while 64% of the men wrote on separate sheets. Taken alone, this may seem trivial, but when we add this to the other differences I found between male and female response strategies, we begin to see clear patterns emerge. Table 2.8 lists the key differences between the ways in which males and females formulated their written responses.

Table 2.8. Differences Between Male and Female
Formulations of Responses

Males	Females
Distance themselves	Attempt to close distance
Use third person	Use first person
Use no dialogue	Establish dialogue
Ask few questions	Ask many questions

Whether their comments were favorable or negative, all of the male instructors kept themselves distanced from the writer, referring to the students in the third person; for example,

I'm not convinced the writer knows what he/she is talking about.

This student is only an average writer but is someone with things to say.

I suspect the writer has been too quick to generalize.

This writer seems to know the paper needs concreteness.

I sense the writer understands the consequences of tone.

But when the female instructors responded (and again, it seemed to make no difference whether they liked the paper or not), 19 (95%) showed a distinct preference for interaction between the writers and themselves—a move toward establishing a dialogue or relationship that was absent in the men. For example, the women would question the writer:

Isn't this jumping the gun a bit?

What do you mean?

Why? Just because you say so?

So why do you want to add to your responsibilities?

The women directly addressed the writer, offering their opinions about strategy or style within the framework of a dialectic.

> You make some fairly good points in this paper, but you seem biased to me, and I found myself wanting to hear the arguments for the other side.

> Please be more careful about mechanics. All the mistakes detract from the effectiveness of your argument.

> You lose me in this paragraph. You have a logic problem. Let's talk.

And the women would offer counterarguments to the statements in the text.

> If a person is unconscious, then *some* judgment has to be made by someone acting in the capacity of a judge.

> What do you girls expect? It takes two.

None of the men offered alternative strategies directly addressed to the writer or gave their own opinion within the structure of a dialogue.

There is a difference, of course, between the task I gave the instructors and an actual classroom situation. But in all of the above responses, the men reacted to this difference; the women did not. Perhaps the men regarded the papers as objects, pieces of work to be considered apart from the writer, while the women considered the authors and papers as more organic wholes. In this situation, women were less able to separate writers from their writing; they addressed the paper as they would the student in conference or in class. The men, however, more readily isolated the texts from the composers. Surely male teachers directly address their students just as female teachers do, but given the text alone, they seemed to opt for a more impersonal stance.

The way the instructors formulated all of the above responses suggests that when they read the student papers, they distanced themselves according to gender in different ways. Like Flynn's and Bleich's readers of literature, the women instructors seemed to identify more strongly with the characters (in this case, the student writer is often the main character in the text) than did the men. Women more frequently responded to the writer's emotional complexity; they were more willing to confront the writer explicitly, and they tried to establish some sort of basis for personal relationship from the start. The male instructors, on the other hand, seemed much more comfortable reading student papers from the perspective of a reader firmly entrenched outside the text, "dominating" the situation (to use Flynn's term) from as detached a stance as possible. Gilligan offers a reason for this difference in the "quality of embeddedness in social interaction and personal relationships that characterizes women's lives in contrast to men's" (8–9). For males, she explains, "separation and individuation are critically tied to identity, since separation from the mother is essential for the development of masculinity" (8). For women, however,

> issues of femininity or feminine identity do not depend on the achievement of separation from the mother or on the progress of individuation. Since masculinity is defined through separation, while femininity is defined through attachment, male gender identity is threatened by intimacy while female gender identity is threatened by separation. Thus males tend to have difficulty with relationships, while females tend to have problems with individuation. (8)

Based on the above, one might be tempted to suggest the innate ability or inclination of the female instructors to join with their students in a complex relationship built on much more than the surface reading of the text, while the male instructors instinctively gravitate toward a more external, impersonal sphere. One could imply that as women read, they are more willing to "share the thoughts of another,"[1] to merge more fully with the "I" of the text than the men ever consciously allow. And one might also suggest that if women view the world in terms of connections and if men see themselves as distinctly separate entities with a reality not predicated on the sense of community that females share, then male instructors might find it more difficult than the female instructors to "suspend the ideas and attitudes that shape [their] own personality"[2] as they explore the world of the student text.

But such interpretations would be inaccurate. Although the teachers did exhibit gender-based differences in the way they formulated their written responses, these differences appeared to have little effect on the substance of those responses: for three out of the four papers, no significant differences between males and females occurred. I believe that because these gender contrasts reflect those

differences noticed by reader-response theorists and feminist critics, it seems plausible to assume that male and female teachers react
differently to student texts as well. But if we keep in mind that the
evaluative context suppresses the influences of gender distinctions
on assessment, a much more probable interpretation will emerge.
We will discuss this in detail in the section titled "How to Be a Hit
with the Girls."

The Oral Responses
    Each interview that I taped lasted about forty-five minutes. I be-
gan each session by having the teachers, four male and four female,
review their written responses and by asking them if there were any
further comments about the four papers they wanted to make. Following accepted interview procedures (see especially Phillips 1966;
and Schatzman and Strauss 1973), I tried to be as nondirective
as possible; after my initial question, I merely nodded my head or
limited my comments to "Uh-huh" or asked, "Would you like to
comment further?" Yet by being an interested listener, I tried to
encourage each instructor to speak freely and comfortably.
    I carefully refrained from using any expression such as boy-girl,
male-female, masculine-feminine, gender, or sex. If the subjects
brought up the issue of gender on their own, I listened intently but
tried to show no more interest in these responses than in any of the
others. When the instructors questioned the nature of the study—
and most did—I explained that I was examining how instructors
respond to student papers, and that seemed to suffice.
    What happened in the interviews was surprising. For the most
part, the teachers merely repeated or expanded upon their written
responses, and no new evidence on gender-based reading differences emerged. But as they spoke, the teachers revealed strong
gender biases and rigid perceptions of how males and females compose. These presuppositions crossed gender lines, with both males
and females responding similarly. But here the effects of gender
took a different twist, for it was not the reader's gender but the
writer's gender that now became significant. (Although this aspect
of gender differences moves beyond the range of this study, interested readers will find a discussion of these responses in Appendix C.) The responses to "How to Be a Hit with the Girls," both
written and oral, also made this shift; however, it is important to

discuss the responses here, because they enhance our discussion on the importance of context.

"How to Be a Hit with the Girls"

With the essay on euthanasia, it is significant to note that if the teachers' responses seemed clearly to stem from gender-related behaviors, the teachers appeared unaware of this; on the surface, they evaluated the paper according to its technical merits. With the "How to Be a Hit with the Girls" essay, however, the role of gender changed. Here gender influences did play a more open part in shaping assessment, but not in ways that provoked gender-based differences. On the contrary, even though the power of gender here was too strong to be silenced, the context was still powerful enough to suppress differences and unify potentially different gender perspectives. Although gender influences were clearly at work here, they affected both sexes in a way that erased, rather than heightened, gender contrasts. We have discussed how the evaluative context diminishes gender-based reading differences. But this context may also be important in diminishing the effects of gender-based presuppositions on assessment. Given the story behind this essay, the teachers might not have subjected it to such uniform condemnation.

While both sexes responded to the "How to Be a Hit with the Girls" essay in similar ways, the paper generated a surprising degree of misunderstanding. In order to catch the satiric thrust of this paper, a reader would need to know the author and the task he set out to perform. Robbed of this context, the teachers were confused and angry, and both males and females reacted in ways they would not necessarily exhibit in their own teaching situations.

Male instructors said:

When I first read "How to Be a Hit with the Girls," I immediately assumed it was a male writer doing it. It *could* be a female writer, in which case I'd admire it more because I see it as a kind of carefully controlled satire, and if it's a female writer writing within a male persona for advice to males, that's even more carefully carried out.

I'd be surprised if a girl wrote this. I'd still have problems with tone and what it says. It would change the reading. I don't quite know how. My guess is that I'd be more favorably disposed to it. I'm not sure. But I tend to sympathize with women when they're writing about these kinds of topics.

The women instructors were equally as candid:

> If this were written by a woman that *would* change my attitude. My approach with the student would be really different.

> Maybe it shouldn't matter, but I don't see gender as something that's not related to the work. I hate to say it, but I think depending on the topic, writers assume a certain credibility or authority. When a man writes about feminist issues, women listen. If a woman had written this paper on stereotypes in advertising, I think it would have less credibility. It would sound like whining.

> It *might* make a difference in the grade if I thought a man wrote this. I'd tend to grade a little higher because I'd be so happy to see it . . . which isn't fair, but I have to trust in myself that I'd address that issue and try to grade it fairly. I try not to treat men and women differently, but stuff like that's real insidious. It just creeps up and I try to keep a real check on it. My inclination would be to grade that paper higher, and I'd be glad to see that a male wrote it because I don't expect that much from them. I expect less from men.

From these responses, it might seem that many teachers are personally offended by certain gender-related topics or issues and cannot grade the students' work objectively. For example, the two gender-dependent papers caused more subjective remarks by both males and females than the two gender-neutral texts. But "How to Be a Hit with the Girls" seemed so blatantly offensive that seven (35%) of the women and four (36%) of the men refused to grade the piece. The men wrote:

> I find this essay offensive from the first line. I don't like this guy, and I'm not the least bit interested in what he has to say.

> I would never grade anything like this.

> I probably would not accept a paper like this.

> Okay, I'll say it. I hate papers like this. Its offensive cultural assumptions are its obvious downfall.

And the women were even more incensed:

> My students would know how offensive I find this. I suppose it's well written, but I really don't care. It's sexist.

> This essay turned my stomach.

> Tasteless and juvenile.

> I can't be unbiased. I can think of *no one* who wouldn't be offended by this.

> No grade. This is ignorant.

> I can't grade this. I'd let the student know it's offensive. What disturbs me is I wonder if my own sexism allows me not to find this acceptable.

> I hate the subject. I need to talk to him about his degradation of women.

A male instructor admitted that sexist papers and politically right wing papers upset him, and he lets his students know that. And a woman confessed: "There's certain things I tell my students I don't want in papers. I don't want sexism. I don't want racism or anti-semitism. I don't want homophobia. I don't want to read these because they're offensive and unintelligent, so I would have a problem with them in that sense. But I also don't want them because they're offensive to *me*." This same instructor, with a higher level of self-reflection than we have seen in other responses, confided:

> I was confused and uncertain about my reaction to the two gender-related papers. They both seemed to have a lot of the same characteristics. But "How to Be a Hit with the Girls" was not up-front about being antifemale. What disturbed me was not really being certain of the reason for being able to grade one and not the other. Was it just me being subjective? It was interesting for me to come up against that feeling because it just made me wonder why I could grade "Tough Guys" and not "Hit." It was upsetting to me because I couldn't be 100% sure. The problem lies in the fact that all the humor in "Hit" is directed toward the girls, without any sense that the author is also making fun of himself.

Only one instructor, a male, recognized the author's ploy and one female instructor saw the author's intent immediately, but confidently assumed the author was a woman attacking males. "It seems real clear to me," she explained, "that this is a woman making a point about the treatment of women." Men, she felt, would never be sensitive enough to write such a piece.

With information about the author and his purpose in writing this essay, misunderstandings such as those above might never have occurred. Given the context, the teachers may have been more sensitive to what the writer was trying to do. One other possible—but related—explanation might be that, unfortunately, we have come not to expect such sophisticated behavior from freshmen as a young male satirizing his peers. Without realizing the background, most freshman writing teachers would probably not see this as one of the writer's options.

In either case, Elliot G. Mishler (1979) would agree, for he insists that research undertaken out of actual context has serious flaws. Data do not necessarily transfer from one situation to another similar one with accuracy or with ease. We cannot assume that teachers reading the texts I supplied would behave the same way with their own students. But when the teachers read these essays, there seemed to be an even larger issue at stake than just displaced context. At least for one paper, not knowing the writer placed the teachers at a real evaluative disadvantage. This could be explained in several ways.

In 1929, I. A. Richards found that readers of poetry often have problems responding to texts from which the authors' names have been removed. Deprived of information about the writer, the readers indicate difficulties in interpreting surface meaning, in understanding authorial intentions, and in avoiding the influences of their own past experience. More and more, readers in these situations revert to stock responses and general critical preconceptions to form opinions of anonymous texts, for if we know who the writer is, we bring to the text all sorts of expectations that may or may not be met. Certainly we saw that with the "How to Be a Hit with the Girls" paper; the teachers could not discern the author's intention and thus misinterpreted the entire piece.

A second possible reason might be that given the lack of information about the author, the teachers created their own author, much as Walter J. Ong (1975) explains occurs when writers create an audience every time they compose. Writers, he suggests, "must construct in [their] imagination, clearly or vaguely, an audience cast in some sort of role—entertainment seekers, reflective sharers of experience . . . and so on" (12). When a writer creates text, he is successful because "he can fictionalize in his imagination an audience he has learned to know not from daily life but from earlier writers who were fictionalizing in their imagination audiences they had learned to know in still earlier writers" (11). Wayne Booth (1961) would concur. An author, he feels, "creates, in short, an image of himself and another image of his reader; he makes his reader as he makes his second self" (138). Given this hypothesis, we have to question what happens to a reader in the reverse situation.

In the human compulsion to order, perhaps the teachers tried to make the situation as realistic as possible. Normally in an evaluative situation such as the one I gave them, the student would be a recognizable presence. Here, the teachers needed to fill that void. With the "Hit" paper, the teachers created a writer who possessed all of the stereotypical qualities society perpetuates, and this fictionalized author, in turn, provoked the sorts of gender-based responses here recorded. Removed from the reality of the context, the teachers reverted to culturally inscribed gender behaviors.

Something else is happening in this study, though, which bears examination. Feminist critics, both those who espouse oppositional reading models and those who opt for a more unifying stance, tell us that men and women read in different ways. But in this project, many of those expected differences did not occur. For example, Schweikart and Kolodny demand that women read with an eye toward protecting feminine concerns. Clearly many of the women did so, and they expressed strong objections to what they saw as a male threat in the "How to Be a Hit with the Girls" essay. But many of the men reacted sharply to this threat to women as well. Although in this case, perhaps because of the topic, both sexes reacted instinctively to sexual biases, for the most part, when teachers read and evaluate student texts, lines between traditional male-female distinctions in reading patterns blur. The strength of the evaluative context moves teachers toward Cixous' and Kennard's state of mutual respect and gender coexistence, and the gender-based influences that occur when readers encounter literary texts cease to be significant.

Conclusion

As teachers, we can make conscious efforts to control our gender-based behaviors or our perceptions about our students' gender behaviors. For example, we may observe through experience that cultural stereotypes often do bear considerable resemblance to the way our male and female students write, and we can make reasonable generalizations based on our awareness and designed to offer our students positive feedback. One man, for example, uses his awareness constructively. "In a sense," he explains, "I try to encourage the men to write personal narratives because I think it's really important for them to explore . . . to write with feeling if they're interested . . . to write with voice and to take risks. I encourage the women, too, but toward pieces more directed outside themselves because they're already naturally inclined to write personal papers." This instructor does set up a positive framework to make the stereotypes he sees work for his students in useful ways. However, he puts forth an interesting paradox, for in trying to destroy the stereotypes, he inadvertently perpetuates them. With all the attention paid to role reversal and freedom of choice in today's society, some stereotypes may be weakened in reality but preserved by stubborn cultural myths. It may no longer be true, for example, that women do not look outside themselves or that men are afraid to be sensitive. But this instructor at least recognizes that some problem exists.

Far more undesirable are those who do see the stereotypes operating and use them to advance bias, or those who never consider at all the basis for their perceptions and penalize their students unconsciously. Dorothy Dinnerstein (1967) notes that "many people do not fit into their assigned boxes, [making] the people who do manage on the whole to stay in such boxes peculiarly unwilling to think about these nonconforming instances in a careful way. A human being who violates rules of gender is violating rules—prescriptive and descriptive—to which most others conform at real inner cost, and around which defensive fear and anger are therefore bound to be mobilized" (183). When students violate teachers' "rules of gender," they should not be categorically disadvantaged.

If I appear to be taking a certain moral stance, it is against those "overreactive" teachers, noticed by Thomas L. Good and Jere

Brophy (1987), who "develop rigid, stereotyped perceptions of their students . . . [and] tend to treat their students as stereotypes rather than as individuals, and . . . are most likely to have negative expectation effects on their students" (137). For example, during one interview in particular, a female teacher admitted that

> sometimes in conference, I feel freedom to be a little more personal with the women students. I check in once in a while and see if I can get a fix on if they're doing okay or if they're having problems. I tend not to do that with male students. On evaluations of women's writing, I'm more subjective, and I'm more objective on men's writing because of that stereotype. I think that's what they want. I know last semester I had six students that had A minus, and I made sure that 50% were women. And that's not to say I fixed my grades, but after I made out my grades, I went back and checked and made sure, and I might have fixed my grades had it not worked out. I might have taken a B plus that could have been an A minus and changed it to an A minus just to be sure. It wouldn't be as much concern to me whether 50% of the A minuses were men.

When teachers remain unaware of these behaviors, their lack of perception often results in self-defeat, as well as in poor learning experiences for their students, especially when gender-based misinterpretations affect student achievement. But I feel that this is the exception rather than the rule, with teachers in conference-based classrooms especially cognizant of interpersonal behavior patterns. Unfortunately, the above teacher's self-awareness has not softened her tendency to polarize males and females, and even within the framework of the evaluative situation, she is unable to recognize the benefits of a more unified perspective.

Limitations

This study, because of its very nature, has limitations. As human beings, our identity revolves around our sense of ourselves as males or females. When we try to study gender, we are inherently incapable of being unbiased; our perceptions continually filter through our own set of gender-based beliefs—those we articulate and those that remain subconscious. Thus, not only must I question my own behavior but the behaviors of those who participated as well. For instance, I have no way of knowing to what extent my own gender influenced the information I received. Would a female instructor have responded to me differently if I had been a male? Would my being male have changed the male instructors' responses? Perhaps by having a male replicate the experiment, these issues could be addressed. In any case, it is important that, recognizing the impossibility of objectivity, we still move on to ask the questions.

Another compelling qualification might be the artificial context of the entire research situation per se. As we have seen, some instructors found it difficult to respond to papers without knowing the student or the terms of the assignment. A project that examines gender-based reading differences within the context of teachers and their own students might yield different information or might reinforce what I have already found. To explore this further, in the next chapter we shall follow two writing teachers through one semester as they respond to their own students' texts.

3

Gender and Writing Teachers: The Maternal Paradigm

IN CHAPTER 2, WE SAW THAT THE GENDER-BASED DIFFERENCES that researchers find in many reading situations did not necessarily occur when writing teachers read student texts. In most cases, the context of the evaluative task was so strong a force that it helped teachers recognize and overcome gender biases and gender-based variations in assessment and in recurrent patterns of concern. However, in some instances, gender distinctions or influences were significant. The differences between the responses of males and the responses of females when they confronted the "female mode" of the euthanasia essay, along with the gender biases that surfaced when the instructors read the dating paper, showed that as the teachers were moved further away from the context of the evaluative task, the power of that context diminished. In this chapter, I will show that when writing teachers who employ a particular kind of pedagogy read their own students' texts, gender-based differences may lose their significance entirely. I refer here specifically to those writing teachers who conference students in a nondirective, supportive way, as Donald M. Murray suggests, and who use a process-based method of teaching.

Before proceeding, I want to define two terms I will be using throughout this chapter: *process* and *maternal*, for I am using them both in a rather specialized way. In the case of *process*, just as there is no one writing process we can point to as a model—for we each have our own individual system of composing—neither do we have a shared definition of process-based teaching. Pointing out that "conceptions of writing as a process vary from theorist to theorist" (527), Lester Faigley (1986) discusses three perspectives on composing:

1. The expressive view
   Including the work of "authentic voice" proponents, such as William Coles, Peter Elbow, Ken Macrorie, and Donald Stewart
2. The cognitive view
   Including the research of those who analyze composing processes, such as Linda Flower, Barry Kroll, and Andrea Lunsford
3. The social view
   Including the work of those who contend that processes of writing are social in character instead of originating within individual writers (527–28)

Although all of these researchers would claim they use a process-based approach, they are involved in different pedagogies, which grow out of their particular philosophical concerns. But whatever their theoretical perspectives, many of these teachers employ similar classroom techniques. In this discussion, the term *process* pertains to these common techniques, rather than to any single theory of process. Thus, teachers who use a process-based method of teaching help students become aware of the process they undergo as they compose; they participate in this process by being interested, responsive listeners and readers; they welcome frequent revisions; and they encourage students to assume responsibility for their own texts.

I suggest that whether one is male or female, to incorporate these two things—conferencing and process-based pedagogy—into one's teaching (and to be successful at it) is to follow maternal patterns of behavior. The dialectic nature of both conferences and process-based teaching shapes a dialogue and a teacher-student relationship modeled on a maternal role. This maternal role, in turn, suppresses the potential negative effects of gender bias and underscores—especially for men—evidence of what Cixous terms our primary bisexuality.

I want to stress here that I am using the term *maternal* in a nonexclusive way to describe any teacher who exhibits those nurturing, caring, supportive qualities traditionally associated with mothering. Thus, in this discussion, one need not be a mother, nor even necessarily a woman, to be referred to as maternal. Rather than an indication of parental status or gender, I see maternal behaviors as evolving naturally from a pedagogical philosophy that embraces sustained conferencing and involvement in process-based learning. In this context, *maternal* applies to males as well as to females.

The idea that maternal behavior patterns can provide models for good teaching is not new. Janet Emig (1983) and Mary Field Belencky, Blythe M. Clinchy, Nancy R. Goldberger, and Jill M. Tarule (1986) have described the possibilities convincingly. I will quote them at length because their ideas are central to our discussion. In speaking about men and women as teachers, Emig argues,

> In my experience, and it may or may not be representative, men teach as a revelation, as an expression of ego. Ego teaching has no use at all if you're trying to teach writing and rhetoric, from any other than a historical aspect. The only ego that should be of interest in the teaching of writing is the ego of the writer, which means the ego of the teacher has somehow to stand aside. In my experience, most men aren't capable of getting out of the way. I think that's the reason there is very poor teaching of writing. I think women, in my experience, are often very, very good teachers of writing because they're willing to put their ego aside. (132–33)

"Teaching writing," she continues, "is more like what is classically the maternal role than the paternal role and that is to make certain that something grows" (133).

Emig refers here to her earlier essay, "The Origins of Rhetoric," in which she interprets Ursula Bellugi and Roger Brown's "Three Processes in the Child's Acquisition of Syntax" (1966), a discussion of how mothers help their children learn to speak. Connecting this process to the teaching of writing, Emig theorizes:

> Why do mothers expand the utterances of their children? Two traditional responses to this question present mother in her usual altruistic and noble guise. The first is that she is trying to serve as translator to the world for her child, that she is preparing his utterance for a life of its own

in the world. The second is that she is teaching her child by providing models into which his syntax can appropriately grow. A quite non-child-centered interpretation could be put on what she is doing through expansions. It could be said that she is expanding her child's utterances for the purpose of understanding him herself. Perhaps adults need a certain amount of uttered syntax . . . and if the speaker/writer does not provide enough, the adult hearer/listener will provide it himself.

What has all this to do with a developmental rhetoric? Mother is the first co-speaker/co-writer. Perhaps the child learns how to expand from the expansions his mother makes in the syntactic sense. But perhaps he learns something more complex, something rhetorical. His mother has, almost simultaneously, served three roles at once: his collaborator in formulation, his reformulator, and his first audience. She is his collaborator because she has expanded a somewhat telegraphic utterance; she is his reformulator for almost the same reason; and she is the first nonself trying to cope with the utterance and help it sustain a life of its own in the world. (59)

What Emig sees here is a possible pattern for mature rhetoric: "(1) the shaping and (2) the reshaping of spoken or written discourse (3) to satisfy the needs of an audience" (59), and she connects this pattern to the role of teachers in a process-based class. If mothers so strongly influence rhetorical development, she asks, could not writing teachers have a similar impact by intervening during the assigning or prewriting stage? "If we can be present," she wonders,

when a student is first formulating his discourse, when it may be in a telegraphic state, we can help him as once his mother did in expanding the discourse—acting, in a sense, as collaborator. We can also immediately be an audience responding as he writes, remembering that flawed or failed writers may be those either who had no significant other (1) participating as they learned to speak or (2) serving as an *immediate* audience expressing with gentle tact and concern the difficulties a trusted audience was having in comprehending the discourse. (59)

Given the extent to which it has been integrated into our writing programs and our own pedagogical philosophies, the process-oriented, conference-based method of teaching writing, which Emig suggested twenty years ago, hardly seems revolutionary today. Most writing teachers accept these ideas at face value. But we may not be familiar with Emig's theoretical underpinning: that this model for successful teaching stems clearly from the maternal role. By not realizing this, we may unconsciously support those feminist theorists, such as Schweikart and Kolodny, who advocate the oppositional perspectives that disconnect our interlocked male-female behaviors. Yet failing to embrace these gender pluralities may substantially weaken our ability to respond to students and their texts with a full measure of effectiveness or sensitivity. Were we aware of Emig's frame of reference, we might develop our maternal tendencies further (this seems especially important for males). If successful teaching is based on maternal patterns, and a conference/process-based pedagogy ideally exploits these patterns, then we should give the most complete expression to our innate maternal behaviors.

Although Belencky et al. do not refer specifically to writing teachers, they also present a model of teaching that takes as its paradigm maternal patterns of behavior. The "mid-wife"-teachers whom they describe share with the conference-based, process-oriented writing teacher those qualities that we have come to recognize as pedagogically sound. Unlike those teachers grounded in Paulo Freire's (1968) "banking concept" of education, in which teachers deposit knowledge into passive students, midwife-teachers "assist students in giving birth to their own ideas, in making their own tacit knowledge explicit and elaborating it" (217). Midwife-teachers encourage students to be active participants in the learning process. As the authors point out, these teachers "support their students' thinking, but they do not do the students' thinking for them or expect the students to think as they do" (218).

Working from Sarah Ruddick's (1980) concept of "maternal thinking," Belencky et al. set forth a three-part hierarchy of concerns central to the midwife-teacher. They explain that

> the primary concern is the preservation of the vulnerable child. The midwife-teacher's first concern is to preserve the student's fragile newborn thoughts, to see that they are born with their truth intact, that they do not turn into acceptable lies. . . . The second concern in maternal thinking is to foster the child's growth . . . [to] support the evolution of their students' thinking.

Midwife-teachers focus not on their own knowledge (as the lecturer does) but on the students' knowledge. They contribute when needed, but it is always clear that the baby is not theirs, but the student's. . . . The cycle is one of confirmation-evocation-confirmation. Midwife-teachers help students deliver their words to the world, and they use their own knowledge to put the students into conversation with other voices—past and present—in the culture.

Once the midwife draws a woman's knowledge out into the world, the third concern of maternal thinking becomes central. Ruddick writes, "The mother must shape natural growth in such a way that her child becomes the sort of child she can appreciate and others can accept." Typically, the mother "takes as the criterion of her success the production of a young adult acceptable to her group." (217–20)

Within the context of our discussion, the parallels between these concerns and our own are clear, for as writing teachers we also seek to preserve our students' new ideas; to foster growth in thinking; to nurture fragile, emerging voices; to encourage active participation in dialogue; and to help students become accepted members of their social and academic communities. On these points, we would all agree. But in general, we may not be aware that the pedagogical methods we embrace have strong maternal precedents.

This unawareness causes two important problems. First, by not recognizing the maternal paradigm, we unconsciously help perpetuate the myth that—in the academic world at least—those qualities that society designates as feminine are not as valuable as those we label masculine, and feminine voices are in effect silenced—thus the long tradition of a predominantly male literary canon and a preference for and a training in male rhetorical modes. However, we must keep in mind that when we do this, we silence not only the feminine in women but also that portion of feminine perception that inscribes the consciousness of men. As writing teachers, we should be disturbed at this cultural suppression of primary bisexuality, for in muting our feminine voices we severely limit our possibilities for full expression.

Second, in their discussions, Emig and Belenky et al. speak, as do most feminist critics, primarily of women. But I see their exclusion of the male as misguided, and I suggest that any dialogue about gender and teaching can—and should—include men, for much of what makes process/conference-based writing teachers of both sexes successful depends upon their awareness of—and their ability to manipulate—their maternal tendencies. Although maternal behaviors seem natural to women, I will show that in the context of process/conference pedagogy, these maternal patterns are equally as ingrained in men.

No one has spoken of these maternal patterns in relation to males. Although Elaine Showalter (1989) does insist that "talking about gender means talking about both women and men" (2) and claims that feminist scholars "need to explore masculinity as well as femininity" (3), the essays in her anthology by both women and men align themselves with the oppositional perspectives we discussed in chapter 1, with males and females pushed toward opposite spheres. But like Kennard's polar reader, writing teachers who allow their gender oppositions to coexist may operate from a richer perspective. If conference/process-based teachers, male as well as female, exhibit maternal behaviors instinctively, then our discussions ought to acknowledge these patterns so that we might learn from them and enhance our teaching.

Research Procedures

In this chapter, I examine teachers' gender-based response patterns in greater depth by considering the reactions of two writing teachers, one female and one male, to their own students' writing. Doing this necessitated a shift in methodology, a move from a quantitative analysis of a large number of teacher responses to a strategy that allowed a more intensive exploration of individual behaviors. Thus I used what Lucy McCormick Calkins (1985) terms a descriptive case study method, drawing on models presented by Emig (1971), C. Stallard (1974), Donald Graves (1973), Nancy Sommers (1979), and Newkirk (1984). Because neither teacher I worked with wrote extensively on student texts, I decided not to alter their natural patterns by asking them to do so. Rather, I relied on oral responses, and I brought a tape recorder to each interview, a tactic that, as Jennifer Brown and Jonathan Sime (1981) point out, provides a permanent verbatim recording of each session. This enabled me to give my full attention to each instructor's responses as we spoke. I also employed a combination of interview techniques that I will describe in the section titled "The Interviews."

The Teachers: Peter and Joanne

The two teachers I worked with, whom I shall refer to as Peter and Joanne, were instructors in a conference-based writing program at a fairly large state university. They were recommended by the head of the freshman writing program as two teachers who were interested in teaching writing and who would support a research project such as the one I proposed. As in my earlier study, neither teacher knew my area of concern. I asked only for their help with an examination of teachers' responses to student texts. Both instructors quickly agreed.

Peter was a graduate teaching assistant enrolled in a doctoral program in British literature. Joanne, a full-time lecturer, held a master's degree in American literature. Both had extensive experience in the teaching of writing: eight years for Joanne, five for Peter. Because their individual expertise and experiences made them such valuable resources, I will describe their educational backgrounds and their teaching philosophies in detail; thus, we can interpret their responses within a fully developed contextual frame.

For Peter, age thirty-three, the teaching of writing was an acquired interest, rising out of the circumstances of working his way through graduate school. British literature was his first love, as reflected in his master's thesis on John Fowles and in his plans for a doctoral dissertation on Thomas Hardy. However, despite his primary concern with literature, he had come to enjoy teaching writing, and his syllabus, as well as his classroom teaching methods, showed a familiarity and a respect for current composition theory and pedagogy.

Besides weekly conferences with each student, Peter employed in-class workshops, placed students in small groups for peer critiques, used in-class writing exercises and written responses to texts as starting points for class discussions and new papers, and encouraged students to revise their work as often as necessary. To this end, he did not assign grades until the end of the semester, although he did evaluate one paper of the student's choosing at midterm. Remarks on student papers were few, often more an indication to himself of issues to discuss in conference than extensive remarks to the student. He did, however, indicate errors in spelling, punctuation, and grammar.

Peter described the chief problems he saw as (1) poor motivation on the students' part, (2) students' lack of confidence, which revealed itself both in lack of knowledge and in uncertain voices, and (3) students' difficulty responding to the full context of texts. Students found it troublesome, he felt, to understand and discuss point of view and tone, as well as to differentiate between fact and opinion.

Joanne, age thirty-eight, had completed a master's thesis on Audre Lorde and maintained a strong interest in women as poets. A poet in her own right, she was keenly aware of the difficulties involved in the creative process, and she saw little inherent difference in composing poetry or prose. Deeply committed to teaching writing as effectively as possible, she had kept current with composition theory, and she had participated in other composition research projects in an effort to help enlarge knowledge in the field.

Like Peter, Joanne ran student-centered classes that depended largely upon peer group workshops, small-group peer critiques, and frequent teacher-student conferences. Students chose their own topics, and they were encouraged to revise frequently. Except for a few editing symbols to note mechanical problems, Joanne did not write on student papers, nor did she assign grades to each draft. At midterm, she spent part of one conference discussing each student's progress; grades were assigned at the end of the semester. As for writing problems, Joanne also saw lack of motivation as primary, followed closely by immaturity and an inability or an unwillingness to participate seriously in group work.

Both teachers considered writing a way of learning, of discovering voice and identity, and of hatching an idea and developing it through. In fact, finding, identifying, and developing ideas seemed the most common crosscurrent in their descriptions of their courses. Moreover, both Peter and Joanne saw the one-to-one conference as their most powerful teaching tool. In these sessions, they acted as responders, as listeners, as coaches—always in a nondirective Murray-oriented way, rather than in the more prescriptive Roger Garrison approach. For each instructor, making sure the students accepted full responsibility both for the conference activities and the direction of the paper was a central concern. In short, Peter and Joanne seemed to have almost identical teaching philosophies and approaches.

Collecting Data

I met with each instructor once a week for the duration of their summer writing courses, eight weeks with Peter, six with Joanne. Peter's was a course in Freshman English. Joanne taught Introduction to Prose Writing, a similar course for which Freshman English was a prerequisite; in other schools this course would probably correspond most closely to a second semester of Freshman English. Although, as I mentioned earlier, both courses resembled each other closely, the main difference seemed to be that Peter taught a research paper at the end of the semester and Joanne did not.

Two weeks before classes began, I interviewed each teacher separately to gather biographical information, to get a sense of how their courses would be set up, and to give them some preliminary instructions. At this time, we arranged a standing weekly appointment, and I asked that each instructor come prepared to discuss their responses to their students' writing the previous week. One way to collect a good mix of all types of responses, I suggested, would be to bring copies of the student essays that best answered the following questions:

1. Which paper did you like best?
2. Which paper did you like least?
3. Which paper was the most difficult to respond to?

Since they had already conferenced the students on these papers, they would be able to describe their responses to the students as well as their responses to the writing itself. We began meeting regularly beginning the second week of class, with one final interview the week after classes ended. Although most weeks each teacher gave responses to three separate papers, on four occasions, three for Peter and one for Joanne, the paper that was the most difficult to respond to was also the one they liked least.

The Interviews

Each interview lasted approximately one hour. I began the sessions by having the teachers give me one copy of the papers they chose for the week and by making sure each paper was correctly labeled (e.g., liked best, liked least, hardest to respond to). Then I asked each instructor to talk about the essays, explaining why they had chosen each piece and how they had reacted to it. As with the interviews I described in chapter 2, I never mentioned the issue of gender or any expression connected with it, such as masculine-feminine, male-female, nor did I show any added interest when these topics arose. When they did bring up gender, I would ask them to clarify a point or to expand on it, but I did this when other issues arose as well so as not to call attention to the topic.

Although each interview had a definite focus—the student papers—I maintained a nondirective stance, allowing the teachers to speak comfortably and freely for as long as they wished. Michael Brenner (1985) sees this neutral positioning of oneself as essential to avoid biasing the informant. Stressing the dynamics of the interview situation, he explains how the unstructured research interview allows respondents to reveal the true richness of their expertise and experience, as opposed to a survey interview in which fixed questions limit the boundaries of response. Robert K. Merton, Marjorie Fiske, and Patricia Kendall (1956) also emphasize the importance of presenting just the right blend of detachment and interest to encourage subjects to provide valuable and sufficient information.[1]

Although all of the above texts informed my research, the work that most influenced my interview techniques is Mishler's *Research Interviewing, Context and Narrative*. Mishler challenges the traditional ways in which research interviews are conducted, both in survey and in more open forms, and he asks for new strategies that recognize that an interview is, ultimately, a form of discourse shaped by both the interviewer and the interviewee. In most conversations, he explains, the speakers share "assumptions, contextual understandings, common knowledge, and reciprocal aims," elements that "allow participants in the flow of ordinary discourse to understand directly and clearly what questions and answers mean" (1). But "in the mainstream tradition," he continues,

> the nature of interviewing as a form of discourse between speakers has been hidden from view by a dense screen of technical procedures. Disconnected from problems of meaning, problems that would necessarily

remain at the forefront of investigative efforts if interviews were understood as discourse, techniques have taken on a life of their own. In this
process attention has shifted radically away from the original purpose of
interviewing as a research method, namely, to understand what respondents mean by what they say in response to our queries and thereby to
arrive at a description of respondents' worlds of meaning that is adequate
to the tasks of . . . theoretical interpretation. (7)

In other words, once we decontextualize discourse as we do in the
traditional research interview, seeing questions and answers merely
as segments of stimulus-response, we lose social, cultural, and personal meaning, which in turn "leads to a variety of problems in the
analysis and interpretation of interview data" (11). Interviews that
follow "a standard schedule that explicitly excludes attention to particular circumstances" do not "provide the necessary contextual
basis for adequate interpretation" (24).[2]
Mishler questions not only the form and context of the interview
but the types of questions asked, as well as the roles the researchers
and respondents play. If, as he points out, researchers present their
respondents with predetermined topics, and "categories for response and evaluation are all introduced, framed, and specified by
interviewers, who determine the adequacy and appropriateness of
responses" (122), then they deny the respondents any participation in analysis and interpretation. Respondents, he urges, should
be encouraged to "find and speak in their own 'voices'" (118), for
"when the balance of power is shifted, respondents are likely to tell
'stories'" (119). This is important, because when people are allowed
to produce narrative accounts, they provide much fuller and much
richer information, less open to the distortion of context-stripping
standard interview schedules. Narratives leave room for interpretation and reflection from the respondent as well as from the interviewer. Thus, rather than following a schedule of preset questions,
I invited Peter and Joanne to talk at length, to develop their own
strands of thought, and to tell their own stories in their own voices.
This method allowed the interview material to emerge as a narrative, which I then analyzed as I would any other narrative account,
looking at how smaller patterns or themes constituted the larger
whole.

The Case Studies: A Discussion

As I listened to the almost seventeen hours of interview tapes and read and reread the transcripts, a key difference between these responses and the responses of the thirty-one teachers we discussed in chapter 2 kept surfacing. The majority of the first set of responses were text based—that is, they concentrated on the form and content of the papers. Peter's and Joanne's responses, however, were writer based—they centered on the problems and progress of the students. For example, only one out of the seven categories in chapter 2, judgments about the writer, referred to students rather than to texts, and this category represented a rather small percentage (7.7%) of the total responses. But in their interviews, Peter spent an average of only six minutes of each hour talking specifically about the essays, while Joanne addressed them directly for an average of only four and one-half minutes of each hour. The rest of the interview was devoted to each teacher's remarks about the students' progress, effort, personalities, and personal circumstances, or to the problems each teacher faced in responding to each student in the best possible way.

A sensible assumption here is that Peter and Joanne knew the writers and could talk about them at length, while the thirty-one teachers I worked with earlier did not know the students and were unable to discuss them with any authority. However, it is important to note how, for these two teachers, involvement in a sustained conference/process-based pedagogy shaped behaviors indicative of a maternal teaching role and helped them to recognize subconscious gender biases. For each, the context of reading and evaluating their own students' texts mitigated the effects of gender differences by making the teachers aware of these differences; only then could they overcome them. In Peter's case (and I expect this would be true in the case of most males because of the assumption that they will not operate in maternal ways), this maternal behavior was illuminating.

Maternal Patterns

For both Peter and Joanne, being conference-based writing teachers evoked response patterns closely akin to those maternal patterns described by Emig (1983) and by Belenky, Clinchy, Goldberger, and Tarule. The teachers they discuss are all, of course, female.

Although we would expect that Joanne, as a woman, would gravitate toward these so-called feminine qualities quite naturally, Peter also instinctively assumed the same maternal behaviors. As he discussed his students and their writing, he consistently upset the findings of gender and reading researchers that male readers distance themselves from texts or "dominate" texts in ways that preclude perceptive, balanced interpretations. In responding to his students' essays, he showed those reading characteristics that gender and reading researchers have found primarily in female readers of literature: an ability, in fact a willingness, to merge with the text in a closely personal way and a tendency to identify with the main character (often, in student essays, the student is the main character), making strong emotional connections. The context of responding to his own students' writing not only suppressed gender-based differences but invited active participation from Peter's feminine perspective.

For example, as early as the second week, it was clear that both Peter and Joanne were establishing nurturing, close relationships with their students. Rather than focusing on the papers, each teacher spent the better part of our interviews discussing the students. Joanne, for instance, mentioned a poignant personal narrative she had chosen for the piece she liked best, but I heard nothing about the paper itself; instead, she told me about the author:

> He's very smart. He makes really interesting comments in class, and he participates a lot. His grandparents came over from Greece. He likes to party, and I think he tries hard to keep up a certain image. He told me he never writes or talks about personal things. But now he's working on something about his grandmother who died, I guess, in the last couple of years. And so he's doing something completely different from his usual. I don't know. He's very sociable and intelligent. I guess that's it. I like him a lot as a student.

She reported a conference that went smoothly, and it was clear that she really cared about whether or not the student succeeded. Moreover, she seemed to have the same interest and wealth of information about her other students as well. During the third week, she described one of her female students:

She's a very eager student, and she's very smart. She's very insightful in her analysis of her own work and also of the other people's work in the class. I mean she really has gotten pretty sophisticated in terms of what she pays attention to in writing now. So that is dominant in her. She is very nervous because she took a class here a couple of years ago and she got a C plus and she had no idea . . . she thought she was doing great. She said it came out of the blue. Who knows? Anyway, from the beginning she's said "Tell me, please, what I'm doing wrong." We had to go through this whole thing where I explained that it's not necessarily that you do things *wrong*. . . . So she's that kind of a student—I mean she puts a lot of effort into the class on all levels. In her own writing, when she revises she does what most students do after two or three tries . . . if they even get what revisions are really all about. She's very dedicated.

In a short period of time, Joanne's account of each student, on both a personal as well as a professional level, had become remarkably detailed and rich. When I asked how she could account for this so early in the semester, she explained that she could not conference students effectively without building up a reserve of caring and trust that depended upon her knowing her students' backgrounds as well as their abilities. Thus, this crucial aspect of her pedagogy—the conference—determined for Joanne a predominantly maternal role.

Peter's central concerns were quite similar. Shattering the stereotype of the distanced male, he showed how important he considered the establishing of close relationships with the author, as well as with the text. Sharing the essay he liked best in week two, he confided:

Well, I like this writer. I'd say she's about twenty-five. She's been working for several years in a camera store. She's married and is returning to school after a long time. She strikes me so far as being very intelligent and very good at following something through. She's probably the sort of person where if she'd had the opportunity to go to college at eighteen would probably be out there with a graduate degree right now. She's very conscientious and a pleasant contributing member of the class— somebody who's doing good work so far.

(I comment that he certainly seems to know a great deal about his students so early in the semester.)

Well, let me say that the comments I make are always very much struc-
tured within the context of teaching composition. I don't think I'm in a
position to generalize. The only thing I will say is that I tend to be somewhat distant as a person anyway. But I think that in many ways I establish
closer personal relationships with the students that I have than I do with
most people I know. In fact, I've just realized as we're talking that sometimes the kind of energy that I put into teaching means that I may be
more distant as a person in other situations. But that's a function of personality. I think in this situation the kinds of behaviors I engage in as a
man are different. There's a clash there.

(I ask him to explain further.)

Well, as I said, I usually don't get close to people. But here I have to. An
inherent problem with teaching composition, particularly with large
numbers like twenty-six, is that inevitably the subjective element, the
personal, does play a part. I mean on some level when you have students
coming for conference and you're dealing on that one-to-one basis and
obviously you're dealing with twenty-six very different people, you try to
treat the students as humanly as possible. That means I have to know
them well. I can say things to one student I can't say to another. At the
beginning of the semester, I'm just flying by instrument. As I get to know
the students better, it gets easier.

Clearly for Peter sustained conferencing demands different sorts
of relationships than he might form in other contexts—relationships
that dissolve many of the myths surrounding his traditional male
behaviors. For example, as Herb Goldberg (1987) points out, in the
business world there is little tolerance for male emotional closeness.
"The autonomous male, the independent strong achiever who can
be counted on to be always in control is still essentially the preferred male image. Success in the working world is predicated on
repression of self. . . . To become a leader requires that one be . . .
undistracted by personal factors" (43). In Peter's situation, however,
the act of conferencing students within a process-oriented pedagogy
reversed expected male stereotypes. Successful conferencing asks
for a moving closer to student and to self, for a certain openness,
and for a fair amount of self-awareness and concern. For Peter, as

well as for Joanne, the starting point of the semester was the establishment of this maternal closeness.

Cixous' vision of inner gender coexistence, like so many other feminist discussions, extends only to women. But Peter's responses indicated behaviors so similar to Joanne's that they demanded to be made part of the conversation. If we remember Cixous' idea of a primary bisexuality, this makes sense, for men are born with the same innate characteristics as women, and as Goldberg points out, each male "develops an intense early identification with his mother and therefore carries within him a strong feminine imprint" (39). For the young male, he explains,

> some of his most profound influences are mother, grandmother, and teacher, who is more often than not a woman. . . . The young boy is therefore being conditioned by the female identity much of the time. As if by magic, by the time he reaches the age of five or six he is expected to become "all boy." The heavy female component in his identity must be repressed. To express it, or to behave in a feminine way, is to open himself up to derisive inferences. . . . To survive in this culture, therefore, the male must disown and deny a major portion of his deepest identification. (86–87)

While the women's liberation movement has made it somewhat easier for women to behave in traditionally masculine ways, Goldberg explains that the male "is still role-rigid, afraid to give expression to the female component in him" (55). However, the circumstance of teaching writing through a conference/process-based method encourages males to voice their inner feminine perspectives. In this situation, they can ignore or suppress the socially constructed gender expectations through which they perceive reality. We can explore this further by considering Peter's reactions to a student text that caused him particular difficulty. We will then look at an essay on drag racing that caused gender-related problems for Joanne.

The Breastfeeding Text

In the third week, Peter had trouble responding to an essay on breastfeeding (see Appendix D). The paper, which begins

After researching breast milk and breastfeeding, and having breastfed for eighteen months, I have reached a conclusion. It is this. Formula, unless under prescription, should be illegal and mothers who opt to bottlefeed, after knowing the facts, ought to be illegal as well. Is this a strong statement? This is only because you haven't read and witnessed what I have. I will do my best in my much too short five pages to win you over to somewhere in the vicinity of my opinion. Let's start with some startling facts.

is crammed with statistics that the author uses somewhat awkwardly to emphasize her feelings that mothers who use bottles cannot possibly love their children. Moreover, the paper is filled with spelling, punctuation, and grammar errors that make the essay hard to read. The many surface errors, as well as the unyielding, angry tone and the very limited viewpoint seem to provide good starting points for a student conference. But Peter was so angered by the piece that he had problems forming his initial response.

When he showed me a copy of the draft, I noticed that his responses were uncharacteristic. As I mentioned earlier, Peter rarely wrote on student texts and then only minimally. But unlike all the other essays, the margins here were filled with Peter's comments, and almost every line had mechanical errors circled or underlined. In addition, none of the comments were the dialogic questions he usually employed. Typical remarks were:

Reword this!

Who says?

If the chore is so easy—*which I doubt*—why don't more people agree with you? You *vastly* oversimplify the issue.

You make no attempt to understand any views but your own.

Although I suspected that his remarks betrayed fairly strong gender biases, Peter himself seemed unaware that this might be guiding his responses. Clearly voicing his annoyance, he explained,

I'm really frustrated here. I don't like this paper. This student is usually fairly conscientious. I know I can't address all of the issues here. Probably it would be most helpful if I made a number of comments about word choice. This student isn't being sensitive enough. She's somewhat confused. I mean, can't she understand that direct address to the reader doesn't always work? This paper is argumentative, and it strikes a very irritating tone. In class, the student isn't really anything like that. She's got strong feelings about this. But this . . . she portrays herself in this paper as a tyrant, and she's not like that in class. Maybe she's rhetorically naive. I guess I'll take the easy way out now rather than saying, "Well, why don't you try something else?" I won't say anything. I don't know what to say. I don't want to deal directly with this paper.

(I ask why.)

Well, maybe she's a bit uncomfortable. Maybe it's kind of a blind spot or something. But it seems to me to be one of those occasions where sometimes it happens when people feel very strongly about an argument—but I didn't say that directly to her. I just didn't know what to say. I couldn't think of one question to ask that would help her out.

The student continued to work on the essay all semester, and each time it surfaced as a revision, Peter would either select it as that week's "most difficult to respond to" or he would show it to me in dismay. As time progressed, he did not seem more at ease with the essay nor did he formulate any response other than the sorts of prescriptive chiding he had exhibited earlier. Each time he brought the paper up, I would ask, "Why do you suppose you're having so much trouble with this piece?" But he would only shrug or repeat his previous complaints.

In the sixth week, Peter was still unhappy with the essay, but now he seemed able to discuss its problems in a different light. Sensing inner gender tensions, he confessed that perhaps his reactions to the essay had more to do with himself than with the writer.

It's not just the topic. That has nothing to do with it. It gets me really upset. Here she makes these sweeping generalizations that you can't be close with your child if you don't breastfeed. She's just not believable. She's had a very good relationship with her children. But so have I. I've gotten up in the middle of the night to feed my daughter. I'm very close to my child. This isn't something that can be laid down by edict. She can't legislate my opinion. I felt annoyed. And defensive. Someway down the line this person made statements about the way I perceived . . . but that was well into the paper and by then I had a strong reaction to it. That doesn't usually happen. It's funny . . . when I told my wife about this paper, she was quite angry too. But I never thought I'd get that angry. Anyway, I had a good talk with the student about revising this. I have to be on guard against this sort of thing again. You know, as a male, I guess I overreacted. I've got to watch that. I thought I was already pretty careful about those things. As you've noticed, I'm a rather largish male, and I've often been classified—to my face—as a dumb jock. So I try to be careful.

Expressing great relief at being able to help the student with revision strategies, Peter—like a writer who needs time to work out problems with a stubborn draft—seemed to have gained enough distance from the essay to talk about the writer's problems rather than his own. And certainly his self-awareness had grown.

Kolodny or Schweikart might say that as a male, Peter would naturally devalue this "female" topic, but there is more going on here. Had Peter encountered these ideas in another context, he might have had the same strong reaction; most probably he would have expressed his anger or impatience and then moved on. However, within the context of sustained conferencing, he had to confront his feelings directly. He had to move past the limitations of his own male experience and find a way to initiate some sort of dialogue between himself and the writer. To do that, he needed to recognize that the source of his resistance to the text might be gender based. Here, the strength of the evaluative context forced him to work the problem through until he could recognize and overcome his gender biases. Only then could he conference the student effectively.

The Drag Racing Essay

Joanne also exhibited gender biases, which the pedagogy she employed allowed her to subdue. We can see this most clearly in her responses to a paper on drag racing. In week three, Joanne was quite distressed at her reaction to this piece. The essay, which begins

"Someday you'll learn about cars. In fact, you'll be the crew chief for a world famous drag racer." If anyone had told me that five years ago I would have laughed hysterically. I was the one who couldn't find the dipstick to check the oil in my own car. I didn't even know how to pump my own gas. Then I married an auto maniac, and suddenly it was either sit in the garage while my husband, Jeff, tinkered on his latest hot rod, or sit in the house alone. I opted for the garage and decided that if I was going to be out there that I might as well learn something.

reveals a woman living in her husband's shadow. Usually quite helpful, this time Joanne had no idea where to begin. Sharing her dismay, she confided,

> I didn't know what to say to her. And *she* was dissatisfied with the paper and was asking me for very specific feedback, and I couldn't give it. And so that was very difficult for me to conference. I mean I kept saying . . . I finally said, "I'm going to take it home and go over it paragraph by paragraph and try to find out what it is that needs work here, but on the surface nothing needs work. The transitions are great. The idea's interesting. See, it's like you set out to do something . . . maybe you could reorganize, maybe you could edit, but there's no major thing that I can pinpoint.

(I ask why she finds this so hard to respond to.)

> I don't know. This is so difficult. I took it home. It took me a while because I first approached it paragraph by paragraph where I looked at the issues and I couldn't see where there were any problems. Yet I couldn't figure it out because I know that oftentimes the problem is that there's nothing wrong with the paper. It's just that it isn't challenging enough. It needs to be more challenging. And so the issue with that is that for some reason I didn't know this time. It wasn't coming to me. And it didn't come to me for a couple of days.

Deciding that the problem with the essay was its lack of complexity, Joanne workshopped the paper in class and not only talked about her reaction with the students but wrote on the copy she returned to the author, "This isn't really complex." When the paper resurfaced with few changes in weeks four and five, Joanne became impatient. Confiding that she did not like the paper and still could not figure out how to discuss it effectively, she chose the essay both weeks as the most difficult to respond to. During the sixth week, however, the writer submitted the essay once more; she had made only some minor surface changes, and Joanne was disappointed. But now she seemed to have made a major breakthrough in confronting the source of her difficulty.

Even though she had not selected the paper as one of her three for the week, she showed it to me and wanted to talk. "Remember," she asked,

> when I didn't know how to respond to this paper? I think that what I realized afterwards was that I wanted her to do something more complex with her relationship to it . . . that that would be the next step. I mean, generally, in a conference, if something is well written, I would still want them to think about it, and usually I have ideas myself. But here I was completely lost. And actually I felt uncomfortable . . . like a classic female like whenever guys are talking about cars and stuff. But then when I thought about it, I thought that the paper wasn't classic female . . . it wasn't so much about car racing as it was about her relationship to her *husband's* car racing. It was kind of the female in the role of helper. So I wouldn't assume it's a classically male topic. I would assume it's a classically female topic. As soon as I realized that, I felt more comfortable.

(I ask if this discomfort occurs often.)

> Well, sometimes I notice it and sometimes I don't. Last week I showed you that paper on economics that I had so much trouble with. I think it might be possible that I had trouble with it because it was classically male. It's something that I've never studied and I'm not interested in. And here was another paper where something was missing from the argument. And so maybe my ignorance of this traditional male topic might have caused the problem. If I knew more about the topic, maybe I could have pinpointed more. But I kept feeling that my ignorance of the topic wasn't my main problem. There was more to it.

When she first began reading the drag racing essay—and the same thing seems to have occurred with the economics paper she mentions—Joanne did not find in the topic any strong source of feminine identification. Had the text been literature, she might have resisted, either judging it unfairly or giving in to instinctive sexual biases. But the context of responding to her student's text allows her to overcome these prejudices, pushing her past surface boundaries she would not cross in other reading situations. After her initial reaction, Joanne perceived that her difficulty in responding to this essay might be gender based, and she was able to articulate her reaction from a more-informed perspective. The strength of the evaluative situation suppressed those gender influences that, given another context, would have prevented an effective response, and Joanne could finally engage her student in dialogue that might lead to constructive revision. The writer of the economics paper she refers to was not as fortunate. Because he did not submit the paper as a revision, Joanne was never given the chance to work her gender biases through.

The Maternal Cycle: Additional Patterns

Fostering Independence

The midwife or maternal teaching model was a strong component of each teacher's pedagogical makeup in ways other than close relationships with their students. Peter was as interested as Joanne in preserving new ideas and in fostering the students' growth by encouraging responsibility. In this regard, nondirectiveness appeared crucial. Each instructor refrained from writing on student texts so that students would realize that they themselves were responsible for revision, and each teacher expected the students to come to each conference prepared to speak about their own problems and questions rather than having the teachers take command. Repeatedly, Peter expressed concern that he give the students enough space to develop independently.

For one young woman in particular, this independence did not come easily. She had written a paper about her job in a camera store, and Peter held himself back from pointing out its lack of focus and direction, because he hoped that she would sense this herself. After a third revision and Peter's patient questioning, she had a real breakthrough. "I'm so glad," he told me excitedly. "If being able to think for herself is the only thing she takes from me, she'll be okay." Describing another student, Peter revealed,

With this student, well, in some sense the context of responding to papers like this is hard for me. It's often harder because his papers seem to be very strong, and it's too easy to make suggestions which can detract from a paper. Particularly because my assumptions are not always right. Usually with a student early in the semester you might think they're capable and they're not. So I'm very careful. I'm aware that I might say something which will immediately be turned into a tablet of stone. In a sense, that might be one of the reasons I hold off . . . because I think there's a chance that I'll add to the problem or the student will misinterpret. I think there's a really strong chance at this point of being negatively directive.

Although Peter seemed pleased when his students began taking risks on their own, he found it difficult not to jump constantly to their rescue. This maternal cycle of supporting and letting go was probably the strongest pedagogical characteristic Peter and Joanne shared.

The Influence of Expectations
While both teachers went out of their way to nurture their students' self-responsibility, their own anticipations often shaped their reactions to a student text. For example, both Peter and Joanne frequently chose as the paper they liked best those essays that reflected the sorts of changes they had envisioned in student conferences or those changes that reflected unusual effort on the students' part. Joanne related,

I liked this paper best because I knew exactly what her writing problems were, and she addressed them. She had been coming to class and doing all the work and all of the in-class writing. And there was a lot she was required to do which she had done. But this paper—while it had a lot of the problems she had in all of her writing—had this clear breakthrough. Like she had very specific images—they were concrete. She had this theme running through it. She was not very successful in using all the images to develop . . . but they were there. I mean, she could have done it. She didn't have the skills to do it, but this was the first time I'd seen her do something that was totally readable. It was an incredible surprise that she had done something like that. I was expecting to be totally muddled as I have been by her writing in the past. So that's why I liked it. I'd seen it before, and I knew what she was trying to do.

And Peter recounted a similar experience.

> For various reasons, I do like this paper. It's interesting—but the main reason is it shows some evidence of thought and energy that comes across. This is at least a second draft of the original, so I'm reasonably familiar with it.
>
> It's quite substantially changed. It still has problems. Still some fractures in the development and flow of the paper. But it seems to me the student has kind of latched on to some of the basic principles about how to communicate with people. I was very pleased. I did respond to the paper and like it through that sort of lens of the student's development and this improved far more than I might have expected it to at this point, which is good. I'm always glad when that happens. Also . . . I don't remember how closely I talked to the student about the paper, but he's certainly done much more than just respond to the details of what I said . . . it seems to me to have kind of indicated that the student has really worked hard on this.

Part of the pleasure Peter and Joanne took in reading student essays seemed to hinge on how much of the previous conference was reflected in the new draft. They realized that their influence upon the students was quite powerful and that given the proper environment, their students would try to meet their expectations. (Emig's description of the importance of maternal influences on syntax acquisition is pertinent here.) But adjusting their expectations to the reality of what their students could actually accomplish was often difficult. Confronting an unsatisfactory revision, Joanne explained, "I thought this one had some potential. But I was put off by the voice and the fact that I felt like it really didn't take much effort to write this. If you knew the student you'd be pretty amazed that she would write something like this—because she's a little older, and you'd expect more. When I talk to her I know I'm talking with an intelligent woman. But I figure that she just slapped this together at the last minute and that makes me mad." And of another student, she confided, "This was her second draft. And it was so easy to predict. I mean I'd seen it once before, and she hardly touched it. I knew what she was trying to do. But there's very little here to illustrate that. As a reader, you have to make all the connections yourself. The problem was very clear, and I thought she understood that."

Once Joanne had invested herself in the text by composing her questions for conference, she expected the student to put forth a parallel effort. Walking a shaky tightrope, she wavered between stressing the student's independence yet keeping a tight thumb on the situation at all times. Having read the text through a veil of evaluative questions, she held in her mind a sort of roadmap—an array of directions the student could choose. If the student stayed put, her disappointment was keen.

Peter often found himself in corresponding circumstances. At one point he explained,

> This student is sort of taking the easy way out. Missed conferences. I've been getting the papers late. You know. Just general sloppiness like taking the paper right off the computer, and she doesn't even bother to separate the pages. She's done work before which certainly shows she's capable of doing more than this. This is pretty thin. Her response is probably genuine, but the paper is—to be honest—the sort of paper I think is written really quickly at the last minute. It lacks vitality. This particular student is just going through the motions. That's not fair. She's not making any extra effort . . . does nothing more than is minimally necessary. And her profile is relatively low in class. She's also missed at least one conference, so I've had less contact with her so I'm unsure about how she'll respond to my response. Had I conferenced her on this I probably would have been more confident in deciding to go a particular way. . . . I don't want to start dissecting this in a way that might not be appropriate.

Like Joanne, Peter expected his students' efforts in the composing of a piece to match his own. About another student he shared,

> I was really aggravated here. Sometimes the conference seems to contribute a lot to the revision, and I like the paper a lot. Here we talked briefly, and the student went away and worked on it. But an incomplete draft came back. We had a fairly good conversation about it and then this. We *did* talk reasonably generally. It's always good when the student can just go away and come back and talk about the kind of changes he made. Whether I like the paper is partly subjective perhaps. It's condi-

tioned by the kind of things that go on in a conference. I don't think there's anything wrong with that, because after a while you can be very enthusiastic about a paper, and it comes back like this one with two commas changed, and you know the student didn't do his part, and you get angry.

As a silent cocomposer, Peter often found his students' lack of effort frustrating, for in failing to hold up their end of the conversation, they destroyed the maternal dialogue he tried to impose. For midwife-teachers, this is a familiar dilemma, for assisting students "in giving birth to their own ideas, in making their own tacit knowledge explicit and elaborating it" (Belencky et al. 217) demands a precarious blend of detachment and control. Thus, allowing students their own mistakes, staying silent when choices seem clear-cut, and remembering how strong an impact teachers (mothers) have on emerging written discourse (language) creates many of the same problems that have plagued mothers through the ages, for it is always the mother whom society points to as refusing to cut the apron strings. For both Peter and Joanne, then, maintaining their roles within the maternal cycle was often a difficult but necessary task.

Gender Differences: Shifting the Context

For the sake of comparison, at the end of the semester, I selected an essay that Joanne had great difficulty responding to and asked Peter to read and react to it. I also asked Joanne to respond to an essay that had given Peter particular problems. I did not tell either teacher where the papers came from or what problems they had caused. I showed Joanne the essay about breastfeeding that we discussed earlier. To Peter, I gave the essay by Joanne's student about drag racing. Removed from the context of reading and evaluating their own students' texts, each teacher responded in ways that reflected traditional bipolar gender oppositions, and their focus shifted from the students to the papers.

Unlike Joanne, Peter immediately liked the essay on racing. After his first reading, he explained, "This one I liked because it was well polished. It seemed to have a good sense of who the reader was. It's a good example of a paper which is focused and specific." But then, expressing discomfort, he revealed a typical male-based distancing.

You know, I learned more about the writer and her relationship to her husband than perhaps I would have wanted to. Obviously it's not my business to say to someone, "You must reveal more of your personal relationship." I *do* know instructors who would respond to this paper as an example of a woman taking a backseat to a man, and that sort of ran through my mind a little bit, and I thought . . . well, it's not the thing I would consider it my place to say to somebody else because, for a variety of reasons . . . well, I've done group workshops in places like 810 [a graduate course on teaching writing]; I've *heard* people say about papers similar to this somewhat subjective feminist reactions which I didn't like. I didn't say anything because it didn't seem relevant.

Obviously I don't think marriage and how you function within that is anybody's business, although as I say I have known people who take it upon themselves to do that. That just ran through my mind. Here's a woman who's obviously being very supportive to her husband and taking this kind of backup role—getting quite a bit out of it, but it's *him* that's winning the prizes. I don't know if anyone else reading this minds that or if it's important. I thought the paper was enjoyable and well done.

Where Joanne's main concern had been to draw out the complexities of her student's marriage from behind the surface narrative, Peter felt it was not his place to do so. Removed from the context of evaluating his own student's text, he preferred to maintain that sense of detachment society sees as proper for the male. When I asked if he would probe further if the student were his own, he hesitated and then said he probably would, but that would be an entirely different situation. "Why?" I asked. He replied, "Because with my own students I have to do different things. I owe it to them not to let my own feelings interfere. I'd probably be happy with the paper the way it is, but if I saw she was trying to write about something deeper and couldn't pull it off, I'd have a responsibility to try to get her to do that."

When he read this essay, Peter made a strategic decision that he might not have made had the student been his own; he chose not to encourage a more personal stance. For Joanne, the task of responding to an outside essay was equally as revealing but in a slightly different way. Upon reading the breastfeeding text, she mentioned problems with spelling, punctuation, and grammar, but surface features aside, she said the text had "possibilities." As a woman, she did not have to deal with the same sorts of gender-based issues that confronted Peter, and she could see the potential in the text without Peter's anger and pain. Although the text had clear problems with development and with tone, Joanne never cited these more global issues. In this instance, the reader's gender repressed flaws in the text. Only when I asked what she would say if this writer were her own student was Joanne able to place her responses within a larger contextual frame and to address the text's shortcomings from a more fully developed perspective.

Conclusion

In this chapter, I have shown how a particular methodology, sustained, nondirective conferencing within the boundaries of a process-based pedagogy, encourages maternal behaviors from both male and female teachers. When combined, these three ingredients—process, conferencing, and maternal patterns—help writing teachers overcome innate gender biases and merge gender-based differences that may be present when they read their own students' texts. Although the conference method seems most important in that it provides sufficient time to establish close connections with the students and to work gender problems through, the fact that the methodology elicits maternal behaviors from males indicates another way in which gender polarities are joined. Thus, inherent in this pedagogy is the natural suppression of the gender-based reading differences that researchers have found in other reading situations. As writing teachers, then, one of our key concerns should be the nurturing of our own maternal instincts.

How can we best accomplish this? In chapter 1, I suggested the need for a self-awareness born of our desire to understand the extent to which we are responsible for any weaknesses or breakdowns in the process of reading and evaluating student texts. A useful first step, then, would be to examine the ways in which we read student texts and to construct a model of reading that could help us study—and restructure, if need be—our gender-based tendencies. If we can begin to understand the ways in which reading student texts differs from, say, reading literature, then perhaps we can respond to particular student texts more effectively.

Some of these differences became apparent during our interviews. Both Peter and Joanne recognized that in their evaluation of student texts they used reading strategies very distinct from those they used in other reading situations. During our second meeting, for example, Joanne mentioned how much easier it was to read novels than to read her students' texts. When I asked why, she replied,

> Because I read student papers looking for ways to improve them, even when they're good. I mean it has to be practically perfect before I wouldn't be reading with a very critical eye. In literature, even when I'm a student, I don't read in the same way. I mean . . . I go much more on gut reaction than I do here. First of all, I have all that stuff that I ask them. What did you like best? What did you like least about your writing? And I'm reading it from that point of view. And then I look for what's good in the paper, because I always tell them to do that. It seems like that's the most important thing . . . like if they did that once they can do it *again*. And then I look for problems that I can question them about in a way that I think would get them to start thinking. I don't necessarily *identify* problems, but I really think about what's missing in this paper and how I can get the student to see that and start thinking about ways to change it.
>
> I can't join with the text in a way that I could with literature, and in a way, I think that's a problem, because sometimes I think . . . you know I read something in a Sunday magazine of a newspaper or a weekly column in a newspaper, and sometimes I think that my students can probably write in that level, and I'm *still* asking them to do something more. So I think it's a weird relationship I have to the writing. It's a relationship I'm used to, because I've been doing it for years, but it doesn't seem like a natural way of reading. It's definitely not the way I read anything else.

(I ask her to explain further.)

> Well, with anything else I just *read* it. I mean, unless it's really poorly written—I guess I just kind of immerse myself in the experience of the reading. I don't read a lot of nonfiction except for criticism of poetry and newspaper editorials. So a lot of what I'm reading for pleasure is fiction. And I think I believe in the writer more when I'm just reading for pleasure—or even if it's something I have to read as a student. You know, I'm not critical. . . . I think the more well written something is in terms

of what *I* consider well written, the less apt I am to do anything but just lose myself in the text. Unless something is really poorly written. Once I start noticing sentence structure or poorly stated ideas or something like that, then I automatically start reading it as a teacher. I'm not *looking* for it, but sometimes something catches my attention, and it just starts happening.

Time and again, as Joanne shared her responses to her students' texts, she revealed how her awareness of this need to question disrupted her normal reading process; she never read the essays for aesthetic pleasure but always in preparation for student conferencing. (For a brief discussion of the term *aesthetic* as opposed to *efferent*, see the section on Louise Rosenblatt in Appendix A.) As she read, she simultaneously formed and reformed questions for herself as well as for the student. Without exception, those papers she identified as the most difficult to respond to were those for which she could not formulate helpful questions.

Probably the most dramatic example of this was her reaction to the drag racing paper we discussed earlier. Once she was able to identify the proper questions to use as an overlay for reading the essay, Joanne could help the student choose a useful strategy for revision. But until then, she seemed to undergo a process similar to some aspects of the writing process, mulling the problem over for a while, allowing the ideas to "cook," to use Peter Elbow's term, until she came to terms with her gender biases. She seemed conscious of—as well as anxious about—an overt split in herself as a reader; for in addition to the reading, she knew she was expected to guide certain aspects of the writing, becoming—in effect—a reader/writer, but being ever careful not to appropriate the text for her own.

Peter also found reading his students' texts more difficult than reading other things. When I asked what the difference was, he explained,

Well, I'd say it's the context. With student papers there's a very definite context. If the paper's a strong one, I can read it and enjoy it. The questions I usually approach a student essay with just fall away. The difference is how much work needs to be done. I think some of the things we have to do it's impossible to do. It's bothering me now. The time available . . . it is *impossible* to do more than try to solve some of the problems. When reading, I try to identify which problem I think might need the most time. That's probably all I can do. When I see a paper that's very well written, I don't need to do very much. When I get to some of the *other* papers I have to say, "Okay, there are several problems here. Do I focus on language? on focus?" I try to read in a practical way. I always have to ask as I begin, "How precise must I be with this student?" Some students you can't say certain things to. It's a question of how much must I tailor my initial response. I always have to ask myself how much of the response is mine and how much of it is what I think the student needs? I'm turning around a lot of papers in a short amount of time. I don't need to do the same kinds of things in such short spaces of time when I'm reading for pleasure.

Peter sensed a multiple consciousness at work when he approached student texts. There was the Peter who wanted to read for pleasure, which was sometimes possible when the writing was strong. But more often than not, this reader competed with a Peter who had to ferret out the right questions to present his students in conference. And this Peter needed to always keep in mind a third consciousness, the student, with whom he must become a partner/composer without appropriating the text for his own. Like Joanne, Peter always chose as the paper he had the most difficulty responding to those essays for which he was unable to formulate the proper questions. As he read, these questions remained central.

In the next chapter, I will consider these patterns further by imagining an ideal model of reading student texts that takes into account those gender variations that might slow down, or prevent entirely, fully effective responses. If we can anticipate undesirable gender perspectives, we can incorporate into our pedagogies more effective strategies for helping our students learn. In chapter 4, I will also consider the pedagogical implications of this study, as well as suggest questions for further research.

4

Gender and Teaching Writing: Conclusions, Implications, and Guidelines

I BEGAN THIS PROJECT WITH A CLEAR GOAL: TO CONNECT THEORY and practice by examining how reader-response theory and feminist criticism—which so influenced the ways in which I had been taught to read and analyze literature—applied to my task of reading and evaluating student writing. However, as I proceeded, it became clear that theory that focuses on the way readers respond to literary texts does not necessarily translate to the rhetorical situation of the classroom. Although this theory may contain interesting and valid implications, things often occur between writing teachers and their students that contradict our strongest expectations about teachers' reading patterns.

It seems to me, then, that this study raises two significant and closely connected cautions. First, we need to recognize that in the field of composition, when we speak of the relationship between theory and practice, we cannot assume a direct transference. In my research, for instance, I found that reader-response theory, while highly suggestive, did not accurately explain teachers' reading behaviors. Rather, issues concerning the reader and gender were played out in terms of the relationship between the teacher and the student. Although reader-response theory proved central to interpreting my data, by itself it could not account for the interaction between teachers and student writing. The theory was essential, but in this context, it could not stand alone; its texture needed the enrichment of classroom experience.

If we extend this thinking one step further, we begin to realize that in our eagerness to establish ourselves as a valid discipline, we must be careful not to stray too far from the source of our strength: our classroom teaching. And a considerable body of writing supports this view. Noting Stephen M. North's (1987) distinctions between "Scholars, Researchers, and Practitioners," Susan Miller (1991) points out that if composition is to overcome its reputation as a field built on "unconsidered practices" and borrowed theories, it needs to consider defining itself in terms of what occurs in the classroom. "While it is necessary," she explains, "if the status of composition is to be improved, that the field promote an academic language and show signs of status that other theorists and scholars can recognize, it does not follow that these two strategies can succeed only when attached to depoliticized, 'pure' research. . . . They need not be divorced from problem solving in specific immediate contexts" (193–94).

Howard B. Tinberg (1991), also critical of theory divorced from the context of teaching, warns us that the "temptation to privilege theory and to devalue classroom practice carries quite an allure" (38). Pointing out that the contrast between "the messiness and the ad hoc nature of the classroom" and "the cool, controlled, and detached perspective of theory" (38) can raise serious doubts about the validity of pedagogy, he suggests that rather than seeing theory and practice as "warring entities," we consider the classroom as a place "that engenders and sustains theory" (39).[1] However, we need to remember that the reverse is not necessarily true; my study clearly demonstrates that theory does not always provide reliable guidelines for pedagogy.

A second caution, then, is that any theory we *do* articulate in composition must be modified in light of—if not *originate* in—classroom practice. Although clearly, reader-response theory holds many clues, we need to understand that our own teaching can be a profound source of guidance. If as a discipline composition is to be given its full due, we must articulate our thinking in terms of concrete pedagogical techniques.

These two cautions contradict Sharon Crowley's (1989) feeling that literary theories rightfully influence the ways in which literature and writing are taught, whether teachers are conscious of this grounding or not. For example, she maintains that deconstructionist theory "presents some interesting models for reading and studying literary texts (and student texts as well), models which might be profitably emulated in reading or writing pedagogy . . . deconstructive insights about teaching, language, and writing offer up a critique on which we can hang much of the pedagogical practice that has been adopted by writing teachers in recent years" (31). Crowley may be correct in stating that writing teachers have often borrowed from various literary theories. And she may also be right in that deconstructionist theory in particular offers a possible model for reading student texts. But by assuming that literary theory is—and should be—the main influence on writing instruction, Crowley perpetuates the tendency to devalue our classroom teaching. We as instructors cannot continue to define ourselves through the perceptions of our colleagues in literature, nor should we presume that any theory we do use need not be reshaped to our own situations. While obviously I am not recommending that we discount literary theory entirely, I *am* suggesting that we resist the temptation to depend too freely upon it to help us interpret our own teaching identity. Our energies now need to move toward articulating theories that arise out of our interactions with our students.

A third key consideration of this study is that in addition to examining our own teaching, we also need to look toward alternative areas for inspiration. It goes without saying that we in composition have always been aware of the relevance of ideas from fields other than literary theory (chapter 1 discusses this in detail). Clearly, however, several spheres have emerged that are central to contemporary composition teaching. Karen Spear (1988) points us toward psychotherapy as a useful vehicle for helping us sharpen our listening, conferencing, and collaborative learning skills. Similarly, Freire's libertarian educational philosophy, with its sources in political revolution, has helped us understand why student-centered classrooms encourage more effective, more self-reliant learners. But even more important, the radical feminist (and I include here Marxist) movement I have referred to throughout this text holds tremendous import for teaching composition in a way that privileges voices that have been up until now silenced or marginalized. Were we to internalize much of what I have referred to as nonoppositional feminist thinking, we would find that the inclination to value theory over pedagogy would diminish. Such a perspective would encourage us to construct theories of teaching writing rooted firmly in our classroom experiences; only in this way can we continue to learn and to grow.

A crucial feature of both Marxist and feminist theory is that they are both concerned with praxis—the unity of theory and practice—as a means to change perceived inequalities. By their very definitions then these theories cannot be divorced from pedagogy. Marxism and feminism speak not only to *what* we teach but also to *how* we teach, and because they do so, they elevate, legitimate, and substantiate classroom practice. Thus they address Miller's and Tinberg's, as well as my own, concerns. But we should be aware that any theory that does this can be threatening to many people in the academic community for whom theory and teaching are divergent forces.

For example, outside of the academic community, I am considered a fairly conservative woman. A product of the fifties, I struggle daily with the ethical and moral changes that have shaped our times. But I find it curious that once I enter the classroom, bringing with me a strong background in Freire, composition theory, feminist criticism, conferencing, and collaborative learning techniques, I am viewed by many of my colleagues as extremist—someone who encourages students to talk to each other; someone who has abandoned her rightful place at the head of the class. Many teachers fear the political shifts that occur in a classroom guided by maternal teaching, equating these shifts with a loss of power they cannot—or will not—allow. Ironically, though, this fear often perpetuates many perceived problems.

To illustrate: in my own institution, as in many others across the country, we are in the midst of discussing curricular changes, especially in the area of encouraging multicultural diversity in both the literary canon and the student body. Yet many faculty members fail to see that *what* we teach is not necessarily as important as *how* we teach, that reshaping the structure of the classroom would, in many cases, solve some of the problems that a lack of multicultural diversity causes. In classrooms taught by the nonoppositional feminists I have described, no student's voice would be silenced; all students would form a community of learners, equal in the opportunity to participate in the learning process.

Within the larger context of my life, my being considered radical as a teacher reminds me that to become concerned with practice often involves risk, and one of the consequences of this risk is that we will meet all sorts of opposition and misunderstanding. But the risk is worth taking. Despite the potential for misconception, we need to continue to look toward Marxist and feminist theory for inspiration, understanding that these ideas are not something we can preach but not practice; they visibly force us to change our teaching.

A fourth important point this study makes is that recognizing the need to construct theories of composition that are rooted in classroom practice also leads us to see that gender has to be looked at within a greater context. But when we try to do this, even seemingly simple issues become problematic. I would like to think, for example, that something so important as gender can be pretty clearly defined. However, trying to pin down an issue as slippery as gender presents as many problems as it does possibilities; gender links with so many other variables that it is almost impossible to isolate. But if we expect to address intelligently, fairly, and compassionately the different perspectives our students bring to us, we need to understand how gender guides our responses, not only to what students say but to how they say it.

A central barrier to this understanding has been, I think, a lingering confusion about what direction gender studies ought to take. By focusing on gender differences, researchers have perpetuated bipolar stereotypes and kept us from realizing the potential maternal teaching has for males as well as for females. In other contexts, the acknowledgment of these differences has been essential in bringing to light previously ignored and/or silent (female) voices. But within the context of teachers responding to student texts, this dynamic reverses. Here, not only does the situation suppress gender differences in response and assessment, but it also suggests that celebrating our gender similarities will strengthen our ability to interact with and evaluate our students in as effective a way as possible. I find this idea of male-female connectedness reassuring, not only because it negates Emig's assertion that men cannot be good writing teachers but because it allows us all certain freedoms of choice and expression that oppositional feminists would deny.

I have already explained how the maternal teaching paradigm I have been suggesting can begin to address issues such as gender discrimination and multicultural diversity in a positive way. Perhaps one day, when we are brought up without socially determined gender biases, we can respond to our students from a more enlightened perspective, avoiding many of the conflicts we now face; and if maternal behaviors ensure successful teaching, we can express them without reserve, whether we are female or male. But until then, we need to find better ways of controlling those negative gender inclinations that might preclude effective responses. Even if ideal circumstances are not possible (e.g., given the student load or unwieldy scheduling, frequent conferencing is unrealistic), there may still be ways to strengthen our awareness of potential difficulties.

But this brings me to a difficult contradiction: gender, no matter how important, cannot remain our sole concern. As we continue to examine how gender shapes our responses to our students and their texts, we must heed Kathleen Weiler's (1988) warning to pay attention to issues of race and class as well. "To ignore class and racial differences in studying gender," she explains, "is to distort the realities of [students'] experience" (50). In trying to enlarge our understanding of gender-based difficulties, we need to remember that culturally much more than gender is at stake. Once we move past theory toward practice, we are forced to confront other complexities.

For example, in my Freshman Composition class this semester, I have twenty-six students—eleven males and fifteen females. I need to be aware that as males and females, these students have very different interests and needs. I also need to be aware of the role my own gender perceptions play as I interact with the students and their texts. But were I to stop there, I would be ignoring other key aspects of these twenty-six people. I do not know, for instance, details such as these students' sexual preferences, economic statuses, family histories, psychological profiles, or exact ages. I do not know if I will *ever* be privy to this information (or, in fact, if I *should* be). But as I look around the room, what I *do* see is that sitting in my class are students of diverse nationalities. On the first day of class, as the students introduce themselves, I learn that two students are from Greece; two are from Jordan; one is from Saudi Arabia; one is from Kuwait; and one each is from Japan, Vietnam, and Cambodia. The class also includes four Caucasian Americans, six Hispanics, and seven black students. Three of the black students are American; the other four are from Haiti, Jamaica, Cape Verde, and Nigeria respectively. And I have to deal with this circumstance. I cannot dismiss the wide scope of difference this internationality suggests—difference in terms of race, of class, of experience, of belief, of religion, of values.

Moreover, in a class such as the one I have described, many distinctions are visible. But for my institution, at least, this class is atypical. I have to wonder what would happen were I to walk into a class of, say, twenty-six *white* students. Would I see only twenty-six males and females? To concentrate only on gender distinctions at the expense of other cultural realities would be an enormous disservice both to the students and to me. I cannot slant my teaching by closing my eyes to all but gender. (At the same time, though, I also think we need to be realistic about how much gender awareness in our classrooms can accomplish. We would be naive to suppose that erasing gender bias in our classrooms would erase the inequities our students face outside of school. Unfortunately, in today's world, males and females are not equal within other social structures.)

I am left, then, with a peculiar frustration. As a responsible feminist, on the one hand, I want to take gender issues into account; on the other hand, I have to acknowledge the sometimes maddening flexibility—or fluidity—that comes with the territory. Because I see gender as an aspect of our selves that raises the most profound questions about our existence, I can only envision a pedagogy that does not take gender into account as seriously limited in its perspective. The problem is not just that we *should* consider gender. The problem is that, as a profession, if we do *not* consider gender, we will not continue to flourish. But we cannot keep thinking that we can look at gender in isolation; further research in gender and composition is going to have to acknowledge that matters of race and class are just as consequential.

Further Implications for Instruction and Research

I have explained that reader-response theorists and gender and reading researchers have explored the gender differences that occur when males and females read literature, but they have not taken into account those gender distinctions that might arise when writing teachers read and evaluate student texts. Although I have shown that, for the most part, the context of the evaluative task suppresses gender biases, we have seen that gender biases *can* emerge when writing teachers confront particular topics or forms or when they read papers by students other than their own. Even under the best of circumstances (in which both male and female teachers operate within a conference/process-oriented context, giving free expression to their maternal voices), gender influences can still disrupt the integrity of the teacher-student exchange.

This has disturbing implications, not the least of which is that given the reality of our crowded semesters, we often might not have the chance to recognize and work through our gender-based problems with response or assessment. Recall, for example, the paper on drag racing that so stymied Joanne. Here subconscious gender biases prevented her from giving the student helpful feedback until the semester was almost over. Or consider the essay on breastfeeding that plagued Peter for almost the entire course. Had he been able to recognize the basis for his strong reaction earlier, he could have spent more time helping the writer to improve. Although suppression of gender bias is neither possible nor desirable, once these biases are recognized, the students are no longer vulnerable to the teacher's anger or confusion. In these two cases, awareness helped Peter and Joanne to deal with their gender-based problems in constructive ways.

Thus, one major implication of this study is that a conference-based course that focuses on the writing process may be the best way of helping us suppress gender biases when we read student texts. In the past, many reasons have been given for teaching writing in a conference-oriented class that emphasizes process. For example, Murray (1968) feels that students learn to write by writing, that only by active participation and practice can they become proficient at their craft. One way to do this, he explains, is to make them aware of their writing process so that they can control it. Murray stresses that sustained conferencing is essential both for better development of ideas and for better drafting. And William Irmscher (1979) would agree. He also urges teacher involvement, stating, "If we are going to help students become better writers, we will have to help them when they most need help . . . [and] concern ourselves with the behavior of human beings in the act of writing" (23).

Joyce Armstrong Carroll (1984) moves a step further by offering statistical proof that training teachers in process actually helps teachers interact more effectively with their students, thus producing better student writing and, surprisingly, better writing from teachers, because they work right along with their students. Her study suggests that writing teachers whose training has been process oriented also become writing researchers; their new perceptions about writing often prompt the teachers to ask new questions and to undertake new investigations. Both students and teachers in process-centered classrooms profit.

However, no one has said that we should employ this pedagogy because it allows us to recognize and deal with gender bias. Yet in this study, I have shown that teachers who read and evaluate student essays within the context of a process/conference-based pedagogy may run less risk of having gender expectations and biases influence their interpretations and assessments. Because they become so familiar with their students' concerns and intentions, teachers who engage in sustained conferencing are less apt to jump to conclusions based on gender stereotypes and expectations, as did the teachers who read the essays on dating.

Moreover, within the framework of a process-oriented course, sustained conferences give rise to those maternal behaviors—such as careful nurturing and support—that we associate with effective teaching. (Keep in mind here that *maternal* is not synonymous with *feminine* and that male, as well as female, teachers can engage in maternal behaviors.) In addition, the "letting go" associated with these maternal behaviors leads students toward independent thinking and self-responsibility. Clearly, the development of these maternal behaviors, together with the minimization of gender-based reading differences are significant reasons for choosing a conference/process-based methodology, wherein the teaching context itself becomes a powerful stimulus for avoiding potential gender problems. One of our research priorities should be to explore ways to encourage and cultivate maternal teaching.

Although I see a conference/process-centered class as one of the best ways to circumvent gender bias, I do understand that for many instructors, time for frequent conferencing may be hard to find. I want to stress, then, that within the framework of a process-centered writing class, there can be ways other than conferencing that allow us to build solid relationships with our students. While brief, in-class conferences may supplant longer, private sessions, journals can also provide a thoughtful medium for conversation. Given the right sorts of questions and responses, we can still come to know our students and their writing problems over a sustained period of time. This carefully developed written dialogue could be a compelling mechanism for encouraging maternal behavior.

My research also suggests that teachers who employ systems that involve blind reading must be particularly careful. For instance, when we read student essays that are not composed by our own students, we often experience the types of gender-based reading difficulties that occur when we read literary texts. We should recognize the limitations of group grading sessions, in which writing teachers meet to discuss student grades, either to train teachers or to calibrate standards for holistic grading. If we read other students' papers as we read literature, we open ourselves to gender-based influences that are usually suppressed when we read our own students' work. This possibility substantially lessens the value of this type of evaluation.

In turn, this raises serious questions about the worth of portfolio grading as a substitute for proficiency exams, a system suggested by Peter Elbow and Pat Belanoff (1986), wherein teachers negotiate "together in a community to make some collaborative judgments" (338). Under this plan, students submit writing portfolios at the end of the semester; these portfolios are read and graded by committees rather than by the students' individual teachers. Elbow and Belanoff see this collaborative effort as useful in setting common standards and working against the isolation teachers often experience during the evaluative process. But this isolation may be necessary to ensure that students receive grades that reflect the amount of progress that has occurred within the framework of the one-to-one conference setting. While I agree with Elbow that evaluation may be somewhat painful, it is imperative that we respond to student papers within a larger context than he suggests. If we read student papers removed from this context, we may expose our reactions to otherwise silent gender distinctions.

Although I see the implications of this discussion for blind-reading situations as particularly important, I want to acknowledge here that the above examples suggest a peculiar paradox. On the one hand, one aspect of our job as writing teachers is to prepare students to write for other audiences. A successful piece of writing must be able to stand alone outside of the context of our classrooms. But on the other hand, we have seen that without knowing the story behind a piece of writing, readers are more apt to misinterpret the writer's intentions. Most of us have anguished at the results of this dilemma, for we can recall times when knowing the background has made grading the essay especially problematic. A student may have struggled heroically with a piece of writing, only to have it still fall short of accepted academic criteria. When this happens, it may be difficult for us to set our awareness of this extra effort aside and evaluate the writing on its own merits. We must acknowledge progress; but we must also maintain standards. For writing teachers who use the process/conference approach, which we have been discussing, the pain (ours as well as the students') accompanying such situations is often keen.

A further implication for instruction rises from our discussion of maternal teaching, which suggests that male writing teachers should develop those qualities that are traditionally labeled feminine. Although successful male teachers, such as Peter, probably already do this, I would guess that many males either act in maternal ways without realizing it, or if they do recognize feminine behaviors in themselves, try to repress them or hide them in an effort to avoid social censure. In "The Androgynous Man," Noel Perrin (1987) tells the story of his "terrifying" discovery at the age of sixteen that he possessed qualities that society labeled "feminine." During a three-day train trip, he conquered boredom by taking a magazine quiz titled "How Masculine/Feminine Are You?" When he finished the test, he was "shocked to find that [he] was barely masculine at all" (209). Years later, he realized that possessing feminine qualities enhanced rather than detracted from his masculinity. Most men, he writes, are "terrified of finding that there may be something wrong with them deep down, some weakness at the heart. To avoid discovering that, they spend their lives acting out the role that the he-man naturally lives" (210). But once men accept their feminine side, he points out, they can enjoy a tremendous sense of freedom. In his own case, he explains, this freedom was expressed in his behavior as a parent.

> I am, among other things, a fairly good natural mother. I like the nurturing role. It makes me feel good to see a child eat—and it turns me to mush to see a 4-year-old holding a glass with both small hands, in order

to drink. I even enjoyed sewing patches on the knees of my daughter Amy's Dr. Dentons when she was at the crawling stage. All that pleasure I would have lost if I had made myself stick to the notion of the paternal role that I started with. (210)

We need to realize that this maternal calling, as it were, also has strong ties to successful teaching, especially the teaching of writing. If males and females could discuss these maternal behaviors openly, this might lead to more effective teaching from both sexes, as well as allowing us to approach student writing from a wider and stronger perspective.

Any discussion about gender carries within it a built-in system of reversals. For example, when we ask whether gender affects our responses to student writing, we also have to ask if gender-based difficulties might arise from the students' perspectives as well. Teachers, of course, do not initiate gender stereotypes. Both teachers and students come to class with long-established cultural beliefs that flourish unless both are forced to reconsider their validity. This raises the question of whether students' perceptions of their teachers and of their teachers' expectations might also be mediated by gender variables. Could gender determine, to some extent, how our students respond to our responses? If students are not comfortable working closely with teachers of a particular gender, would that prevent them from learning and improving? An exploration of this within the context of a writing class could prove valuable.

Some implications of this discussion move beyond the writing classroom and suggest that some feminist theorists may encourage gender differential behaviors that are not very constructive. I refer here to those feminist critics we have discussed, such as Gardiner, Schweikart, and Kolodny, who talk about male-female concerns in terms of oppositional perspectives. Unfortunately, we have seen that in writing classes these oppositional perspectives can have negative consequences. For example, recall the female instructor in chapter 2 who told the story about altering grades so that the women in her class would have as many A grades as the men. Clearly, practices of this sort should have no place in our writing classes. But this incident suggests, too, that in other areas of feminist academia, oppositional perspectives might be encouraging unfair behaviors toward male students.

Oppositional feminism invites polarities and discourages the relationships male and female teachers might build with their colleagues and students of the opposite sex. Particularly ironic is that they also inhibit any feminine tendencies males might exhibit, making desirable maternal teaching behaviors less accessible. A more useful body of research would examine how to strengthen, rather than how to sever, male-female connections. It seems to me that the unifying perspectives of Kennard and Cixous would better serve the interests of everyone involved. By insisting that we not summarily dismiss difference, these two writers push us toward the realization that each gender, by its very definition, has a certain innate worth. In a classroom guided by nonoppositional feminism, the limitations that derive from gender stereotypes quickly give way to acceptance, dialogue, flexibility, self-awareness, tolerance, and understanding. Clearly, in such an atmosphere, negative gender influences cannot survive.

Responsive Reading: Theoretical Foundations

I have been suggesting that as we read student texts, we can suppress the effects of gender bias by paying careful attention to our classroom experiences and behaviors. A prime concern then is how to foster a better understanding of the gender issues that often help shape our responses. One way to do this would be to look a bit further at some of the reading theories we have discussed, for they raise key questions about how gender operates within the context of teachers evaluating student texts and lay the foundation for what I call *responsive reading*.

Unlike critical reading (during which we concern ourselves with discussing or evaluating the form and/or content of the text), Rosenblatt's aesthetic reading (reading for pleasure), or her efferent mode (reading for information), responsive reading occurs when, as writing teachers, we read with an eye toward providing the sorts of supportive feedback and dialectic exchange that will encourage our student writers to think for themselves and to revise effectively. With unbiased (to whatever extent that is possible) responsive reading, our scope enlarges to include a special awareness of possible gender inequities as we read within the framework of the evaluative task. To understand more clearly how this might work, let us review briefly those reading theories that fall into three broad categories: reader response, oppositional feminism, and nonoppositional feminism. From each of these areas, I have derived a set of guidelines for responsive reading

Reader-Response Theories

As I point out in chapter 1, the three reader-response theorists especially pertinent to this study are Culler, Bleich, and Holland. Noting that feminist critics wonder whether males and females can value literary works authored by the opposite sex, Culler raises, by implication, three important questions for our teaching:

1. Given their own experience, do male writing teachers devalue the topics and forms their female students choose?
2. Is the reverse true? Do female teachers devalue their male students' texts?
3. Do we have preconceived gender attitudes toward our students of which we need to be aware?

We have seen that although the answer to all three questions can be yes, gender influences can be mitigated given a certain pedagogical situation. Culler is important because, as one of the first to question the issue of gender, he sets up a foundation for further investigation. Once we acknowledge the validity of the questions he suggests, we are drawn into an examination of our own behaviors. Clearly, this self-examination is a critical first step toward establishing a set of responsive reading guidelines.

Bleich and Holland join Culler in reminding us implicitly that as readers we play an important role in interpreting student texts. Demonstrating how males, because of the separation problems involved in their attaining gender identity, remain more distant from literary texts than women, Bleich leads us to question how our gender affects our own relationships to student texts. In chapter 2, we found strong examples of gender-based problems with form and topic, as well as with distance, both in relation to texts and to students. In addition, Holland's work suggests that when we read, we look for elements in a text that reflect portions of our own identities. Thus, male reading patterns may not help male teachers negotiate female texts, and vice versa. With certain essays, such as the ones we read on dating, we saw that we can sometimes subconsciously penalize our students for not re-creating our identity themes.

What joins Culler's, Bleich's, and Holland's work is their insistence that the reader creates the text, that the experience of reading is primary to interpretation, that the reader—not the author—controls the text regardless of what is actually written on the page. The text, they say, is an object upon which we perform our own subjective actions; the writer loses significance. But here is where these theorists seem to part company with the circumstance of teachers reading student texts.

At first glance, when we consider how writing teachers read student essays, reader-response theory does not appear relevant. Although historically, writing teachers have concentrated on the final product, in the last few decades, we have come to realize that being involved in the students' writing process, focusing on their questions and problems as they write, is a more effective way to help students learn. In this context, the writer, rather than the reader or the text, is central; our own subjective responses are not the main focus of our concern. Thus, our determination as teachers to bury the subjective response, to take every precaution to avoid appropriating the text as our own is quite the opposite of what these critics say occurs when text and reader meet.

But I think as instructors we should be paying closer attention to what reader-response theorists are saying. Perhaps part of our reluctance to acknowledge the subjective stems from that portion of our training in literary criticism that dealt with the affective fallacy, W. K. Wimsatt's (1954) famous warning to avoid confusion between a poem and its results. However, I suggest that in our quest for objectivity, we miss a much-needed chance to open up the subjective realm and examine it. In doing so, we close off a rich source of information about how we interpret and evaluate student writing. The gap between what we feel as we read and what we are willing, or able, to admit needs to be carefully considered so that we can better understand the reasons behind our responses.

This hesitation—or inability—to acknowledge the subjective presents a sticky problem. On the one hand, reader-response theory seems so sensible. Since each of us perceives reality (texts) differently, it seems logical to examine what specifically within each of us determines textual interpretation. If everyone creates his or her own text, then the authority of the reader supersedes that of the author; in fact, the author, in effect, disappears as a determining force entirely. But when teachers read student texts, they do so at the will—and at the service—of the writer. If the writer as a force determining meaning were to disappear, there would be no reason to read the text in the first place. Hence, we have to make some compromises. Especially in a maternal teaching situation, where we are concerned chiefly with nurturing confident, independent thinking, the primacy of the writer must be maintained.

What, then, can we as writing teachers appropriate from reader-response criticism as part of our guidelines for responsive reading? Traditionally, when we read and evaluate student texts, we concentrate on the student and on the writing. I suggest that as we read student texts we acknowledge the important contributions of all *three* participants: the reader, the writer, and the text. In our attempts to help the student revise the text effectively, we should pay attention not just to the student's needs or to the text's strengths and weaknesses but also to those ingredients in our own interpretations that might stem from subconscious gender biases. In doing so, we enlarge the basis for our evaluations and extend our potential for more informed, and perhaps more helpful, responses. Thus, a first step when we begin reading a student essay might be to anticipate signs of gender influence and to critically reevaluate any strong initial reactions we might have that cannot be explained. Step two develops from our discussion of oppositional feminism, while steps three and four spring from the work of Kennard and Cixous.

Oppositional Feminism

In addition to reader-response theory, feminist criticism suggests other ways in which we can examine our subjective responses to student texts. Although we have seen that oppositional feminists encourage implicitly those male-female polarities that cause many gender-based reading problems, we can still find parts of their theory useful. In particular, Kolodny and Schweikart augment and clarify elements of reader-response criticism. In chapter 1, we saw that as she reads, Kolodny (1982) looks for validations of feminine significance asking two key questions:

1. How do contemporary women's lives, women's concerns, or concerns about women constitute part of the historical context for this work?

2. What is the symbolic significance of gender in this text? (175)

By setting up the activity of reading as a direct gender confrontation, Kolodny excludes men from her community of readers. We must disqualify her first question as too limiting, partly because we owe equal allegiance to our male students and partly because this project is as concerned with male teachers as it is with females. But were we to amend the gender in the second question to include men, we would see how strongly she reinforces our first guideline. Her work prods us to remember that as we examine the relationship between our responses and the student text, we can try to determine whether gender signals in the text (or in our selves) have triggered any of our emotional as well as intellectual reactions.

Schweikart's theory of subjective doubling helps us even further by reminding us, as reader-response theorists have done already, how fragile is any illusion of objectivity during the reading process. But Schweikart moves beyond reader-response theorists by pointing out their male preoccupation with "issues of control and partition—how to distinguish the contribution of the author/text from the contribution of the reader" (55). She explains that in feminist patterns of reading, control of the text is not at issue. Rather, a woman's interest is to "connect," to "negotiate between opposing needs so that the relationship can be maintained" (55). Thus, instead of taking control of a text, a female wants to take control of her own reactions to it.

This is a crucial difference, for it reinforces my contention that we need to explore the subjective realm. We cannot take control of our own reactions unless are aware of them in the first place. But in addition, it seems to me that Schweikart's dialectic model of reading can be an important source of information in another way. While centered on a female paradigm of reading literature, her model suggests the sorts of reading experiences both male and female teachers encounter when they read student texts within the parameters of a conference-based writing course. Schweikart describes a way of reading based on respect for the autonomy of the text, with the

reader ever wary of "unwarranted intrusions," careful not to "appropriate what belongs to" the writer or to "impose herself" in any way
(48). For her, reading is "an intersubjective encounter" dependent
upon "the need to connect" with the writer in a very personal, as
well as a protective, way (48). She sees reading as a series of three
dialectic "moments":

1. Subjective doubling, the recognition by the reader that she is
   responsible for giving meaning to someone else's words.
2. The realization that this illusory doubling of subjectivity is difficult to maintain in the absence of the author.
3. The need to prevent total subjectivity by mediating one's own
   experience between the context of writing and reading, without appropriating the text entirely.

To we teachers who employ nondirective conferencing, Schweikart's paradigm must seem familiar, for the success of these sorts of
encounters depends, to a great extent, upon our willingness not to
appropriate the student's text and not to impose our own ideas about
what direction a new draft should take. Instead, we respect the student's intentions and concerns, and we try to encourage independent thinking. To do this, we must connect with a subjectivity other
than our own, and we must recognize and meet the needs of this
other subjectivity.

In many ways, accommodating another subjectivity should be
easier for a writing teacher than it is for a reader of literature, for
our students are very present, not just extensions of our own subjectivity; and in writing courses, our students, not we ourselves, are
responsible for making meaning. Those of us who work within a
conference-based course have the luxury of actual conversation with
the writers. This provides the safeguards (which Schweikart claims
are absent in other reading situations) whereby we can preserve the
duality of reader-writer, insulating, or protecting, the writer from
our own subjectivity. Especially when gender issues threaten un-
due influence, remembering Schweikart's "moments" could help us
preserve this duality more easily and keep us from appropriating
the text.

We can use Schweikart's pattern to consider how gender influences work within the boundaries of teacher/student dialogues. For
example, when Peter read the breastfeeding essay (I return to this

example now and further on in this discussion, because it so powerfully demonstrates the scope of gender's effect upon our reading), his highly charged emotional reaction clouded his ability to consider the writer's needs. Instead of realizing the extent to which he himself was responsible for giving meaning to the author's words, he accepted his singular response at face value. His anger, rather than the writer, became his primary concern. Had he recognized the crucial role of his own subjectivity, he could have seen that his own role in the reading process was just as powerful as the role played by the text. And this recognition could have helped him move toward what Schweikart calls "genuine intersubjective communication" (53), a dialectic that demands, and honors, the duality of reader and author. In achieving this, Peter could have acknowledged a subjectivity separate from his own (even though as he read, this doubling would be taking place *within* him), and he could have begun the dialogue necessary for preventing his own subjectivity from taking over entirely. His own self-awareness could have helped him take control of his response, and he could have started "connecting" with the writer in a positive way. A second guideline then might be to incorporate into our reading patterns an awareness of how subjective doubling allows us to negotiate meaning without imposing upon the text our gender-based biases or preconceptions.

Nonoppositional Feminism

With their attempt to unite traditional male-female binary oppositions, Kennard and Cixous offer us, by implication, concrete strategies for dispelling gender conflicts when we read student texts. Urging a respect for both aspects of one's self, Kennard encourages a healthy acknowledgment of one's male-female contraries and maintains that a successful reading deliberately "allows the polarities to coexist" (70). In our discussion of maternal teaching, we saw how this acceptance and combining of oppositional forces within Peter was essential to his success with his students, especially in gender sensitive situations. Thus this "leaning into" those texts that might pose gender-based problems with response and assessment provides us a third guideline. As we read and evaluate student texts, we need to listen to our inner male-female voices, being especially sensitive to signs of gender suppression. If, for example, we notice ourselves resisting a text, we might want to examine whether or not the grounds for that resistance might be gender based. Are we expressing one element of our gender identity at the expense of the other? Are we repressing either our masculine or our feminine inclinations? For males, this question seems particularly important.

Finally, in Cixous we find a powerful indication for our model of responsive reading, for she describes herself as a reader never separated from her "other"—which for her refers to the writer as well as to the double-gendered consciousness within. Although she, too, writes from a feminist perspective, her joyous celebration of inner gender coexistence allows for the inclusion of males and offers a way of looking at the world—a way of reading, as it were—which, as I noted earlier, promises to cancel bipolar gender limitations.

Cixous is important to our discussion for several reasons. First, as writing teachers, we too find ourselves unable to confront a student text without also confronting our other. Although traditionally, for teachers, this other has always been the writer, by acknowledging two additional doubles—ourselves as reader-writer and ourselves as male-female—we can strengthen our responses by bringing to the student, and to the text, an enriched basis of understanding and concerns. For women, this could mean a less-limiting perspective, an ability—and a willingness—to accept male strategies and perceptions on their own terms, without regarding all traces of the masculine as automatic assaults on feminine sensibility. For men, new insights about their inner feminine could enhance those maternal behaviors that, as we have seen, lie behind much successful teaching.

Perhaps even more important is Cixous' description of reading as a continuous action between the reader and the page, with the reader ever in control, ever shaping or transforming the text, yet respecting always the presence of the writer. For her, maintaining the integrity of reader, writer, and text is central; yet she never privileges one at the expense of silencing any other. Unlike traditional, Western feminists, Cixous values the text and the activity of reading for the gender connections they promote, rather than for the disunity most feminist readers see as central to the undertaking. Sympathizing with perceptions foreign to her in terms of gender, she discourages the gender polarities that underlie many of the reading difficulties we have discussed so far. While other feminists see the tearing down of male values as a key operating concept,

Cixous realizes that only by preserving elements of both genders can any reading—or reader—gain success.

It seems obvious that as writing teachers we would have much to gain by adapting Cixous' precepts to our own tasks. If Peter and Joanne, for example, had internalized as part of their reading patterns Cixous' distaste for gender polarities, they might have accepted more easily those essays that caused gender-based difficulties. At the very least, their attention would have shifted sooner to the reasons behind their strong reactions. As a fourth guideline, then, let us say that when we read student texts, we should sympathize with and respect gender perceptions opposite from our own, taking care not to privilege one gender at the expense of the other. Thus can we insure both male and female students of equitable responses.

The following list presents a summary of the guidelines we have been discussing. Although at first glance, most of these guidelines might seem rather obvious, they are important to keep in mind because we usually concentrate either on our students or on their texts, paying little attention to our own behaviors. But only when we make these behaviors conscious, can we try to change them. I suggest that following these guidelines would decrease substantially those response problems that we often may not recognize as being gender based. I acknowledge that given the sometimes overwhelming numbers of student essays that we must respond to, adding four questions to our already crowded repertoire might seem burdensome. But in truth, internalizing them and becoming alert to gender stimuli could help us respond to students more efficiently. Let us consider how supplementing Peter's and Joanne's approach to student essays with the following guidelines would have prevented many of the barriers to interpretation caused by their subconscious gender biases.

Guidelines for Responses to Student Texts
1. Anticipate signs of gender influence and critically reevaluate any strong initial reactions we might have that cannot be explained otherwise
2. Incorporate into our reading patterns an awareness of how subjective doubling allows us to negotiate meaning without imposing upon the text our gender-based biases or preconceptions

3. Listen to our inner male-female voices, being especially sensitive to signs of gender suppression
4. Sympathize with and respect gender perceptions opposite from our own, taking care not to privilege one gender at the expense of the other

Responsive Reading: Practical Applications

For teachers who work within the framework of a conference/process-oriented class, how to respond to students in conference most effectively is, of course, a central concern. As Peter and Joanne both explained, the context of reading and evaluating student essays demands different reading patterns than those they employ in other situations. In evaluating, they approach the text through a grid of questions aimed toward shaping a dialectic exchange. Thus, in addition to matters of content and form, they anticipate the conference (e.g., What advice or questions will most help this student see the text's strengths and weaknesses? How should these questions or suggestions be presented? How should I shape my response to help the student revise effectively? What questions will best help this student develop his or her thoughts further? How supportive can I be while still being constructively critical?). Recall that when gender influences interfered with the formation of these questions, both Peter and Joanne expressed a deep sense of concern and frustration.

As Peter read the essay on breastfeeding, he encountered great difficulty, not only with his reactions to the text but also with his ability to communicate with the writer. Had he been aware that gender was such a significant motive for his reactions, he could have utilized some of the guidelines to help him work through his problem in responding. Although at first this might mean using the guidelines as a sort of checklist, once he internalized them, they would become a spontaneous part of his responsive-reading pattern.

To illustrate: Peter's strong, negative reaction to the essay should have acted as a warning signal that something out of the ordinary was happening as he read. Surely other students turned in writing that was as undeveloped, as opinionated, and as abrasive in tone. In fact, he had shown such examples to me during the semester. But this particular essay aroused an anger and an impatience seemingly out of proportion as well as out of character. A good strategy here would have been to try to discover the reasons behind his reaction. While Peter spent a good deal of time wrestling with the text and arguing with the writer, a more useful technique would have been to examine his own role in this drama for signs of gender bias. A careful appraisal of any one of the four guidelines would have suggested that he look within for the source of the problem. For instance, he might have asked himself whether he felt uncomfortable with the paper's main premise: that only through breastfeeding can parental closeness be attained. As a male, he might certainly have felt excluded by this contention; and as a father who considered himself close with his young child, this sense of exclusion may have extended to the sense of denial and anger that prevented him from engaging the writer in constructive dialogue. Clearly, as the semester progressed, he began to notice these possibilities, and he was able to deal with them more evenly.

For Joanne, the realization that gender bias might be influencing her reactions was just as difficult. Unable to formulate any concrete reaction to the drag racing essay, she assumed the problem might lie in the paper's lack of complexity or in the author's refusal to transform the essay into an intimate examination of her marriage. Confused, Joanne found herself stalling, taking the paper home, discussing it in class workshop, hoping to get some handle on the source of her uneasiness. Because as she read she searched for signs of a feminist sensibility, she was unable to value the limits of the writer's awareness. If she had questioned whether her own strong feeling about a woman's place within marriage was preventing her from achieving the subjective doubling necessary to inhibit total subjectivity, Joanne might have realized sooner that she was trying to manipulate the text, changing the writer's intention to align more tightly with her own feminist stance. Fettered by her own perception of proper female behavior, she concentrated on the paper's limitations and on the writer's inability to share her point of view rather than on her own problem in responding effectively. In this instance, Joanne—and her student—would have benefited greatly from Joanne's early recognizing of the origin of her difficulty.

The guidelines for responsive reading call for better monitoring and understanding of our behavior as teachers. This is consistent with the general thrust of reader-response criticism, which describes and analyzes the ways in which we perceive and interpret texts. Reader-response theorists also ask us to realize our own important roles as producers of meaning and, by implication, as members of a complex rhetorical relationship with our students. Once we shift our emphasis from the students and their texts to ourselves, we can see the effects of our gender-based reading differences, and we can minimize any negative influences on response and assessment.

Other researchers have also commented upon the importance of self-awareness for teachers, albeit in other teaching situations. They have noticed, for example, that teachers spend much time and energy guiding and evaluating their students, without paying much attention to their own pedagogical practices. Graves (1981) points out the need for this new focus, explaining that we have "never actually studied the process of teaching writing" (102) as we have the process of writing itself. But this self-examination, he stresses, is crucial for better teaching.

Perhaps we should translate this call for self-awareness into better training programs for our future teachers. For instance, Good and Brophy would agree that many teachers remain unaware of their pedagogical behavior and its effects. They cite two primary reasons why we often fail to recognize how we influence our students. First, they explain, "the most fundamental factor making it difficult for teachers to assess [their] behavior is that so much happens so rapidly that they cannot be aware of everything they do. This problem can be solved in part through training. Awareness of everything that occurs is impossible, but with practice teachers can become more aware of their . . . behavior" (43). Their second point centers on teacher-training programs, which rarely "provide [teachers] with skills for analyzing and labeling [their] behavior. . . . Most in-service teachers are not able to describe accurately what occurs" (43). Good and Brophy suggest that teacher-training institutions and in-service programs need to find ways to show teachers how to label and monitor their behavior.

Even more significant for our discussion, G. Leinhardt, A. M. Seewald, and M. Engel (1979) documented teachers' differential behaviors toward male and female students but found that the teachers were not aware of treating their male and female students differently. Thus, we have to wonder if when we enter the writing class our lack of awareness about gender-based influences could damage our relationships with our students and prevent us from assessing their work fairly. In short, we might not realize the extent to which gender might be shaping our responses. Adopting the guidelines for responsive reading would help us gain the self-consciousness that these researchers claim is central to good teaching.

Another well-established body of work reinforces the importance of self-awareness even further. Teachers may be reacting to very real distinctions between male and female students' texts. We have already discussed Farrell's male and female modes of writing (see chapter 2), and we have seen that the differences between these two modes might have been responsible for the significant discrepancies between male and female evaluations of the essay on euthanasia. Other studies on male-female distinctions support this finding. For example, Graves (1973) found developmentally based sex differences in seven-year-old boys and girls and noted that the thematic choices boys made varied considerably from the choices of girls. Boys wrote more about exploring, traveling, dealing with the broader world, while girls wrote more about the family, the classroom, themselves.

Anne Sherrill (1979) monitored the thematic choices of seventh and tenth graders and college freshmen and arrived at findings similar to Graves'. She noticed that as students get older, the differences between the sexes narrows, but they still exist. College-age females seem more able to write about themselves and their feelings than college-age males. In the same vein, Margaret B. Piggott (1979) observed that this clear preference in topic choices alone indicates that men avoid personal references, while women feel decidedly more comfortable writing about themselves.

Janet White (1984) also found that girls are more likely to write about themselves and their relationships with friends and family, while boys seem more at ease with subjects more external to themselves, such as sports. Jo Keroes (1987), however, saw in a study of college-age writers that while women are more likely than men to write about issues of relationships and connectedness, overall both male and female college-age writers choose more autonomous subjects.

Barbara L. Cambridge (1987) and Cinthia Gannett (1987) also examine male and female writers in terms of the types of writing they do. Cambridge feels that men and women enter the freshman writing class with different interactional dispositions that are evident both in their writing and in their speech. She urges writing teachers to become aware of these differences with the aim of supporting the ideas and expression of both genders. Gannett finds striking differences between the quantity and quality of journal writing done by male and female student writers and discusses how the journal writing of her students reveals gender-preferential reading and writing strategies.[2]

These researchers consider gender differences in student texts and behaviors. My own work indicates that this research should shift a bit to include the pedagogical behaviors that might arise in reaction to these student differences. Doing this, in conjunction with using the guidelines for responsive reading, might eliminate the negative effects of gender almost completely and help us to expose inbred cultural assumptions about males and females, which have become so comfortable that we often fail to notice them.

My findings also suggest that the guidelines for responsive reading could benefit student readers of poetry and literature. Bleich's and Flynn's research implies not only that males and females read differently but that females are, in effect, often better readers, because they can join with a text more closely than males, who try to maintain a certain control and distance. If readers of both sexes can understand how gender may dictate their initial emotional responses, they may be able to use that knowledge to analyze texts more effectively. One way to accomplish this would be to train student readers to incorporate the guidelines for responsive reading into their reading patterns. This could help them overcome any gender biases that might prevent useful interpretations.

I have argued that given a set of guidelines for responsive reading, writing teachers can overcome the gender-based difficulties that often arise when they read student texts that challenge their gender beliefs and/or expectations. To do this, they need to keep alert to signs of gender influence or bias that might prevent either fair assessments or useful dialectic conferencing. Although at first this effort would be highly conscious, it seems logical that in time the gender guidelines for responsive reading would become a key, internalized ingredient of our reading behaviors. In this way, perhaps many of the gender inequities that concern us in other situations can be filtered out of our responses to student writing, and gender biases will cease to operate as significant factors.

Conclusion

The forces that shape our gender perceptions are deeply rooted in our social, political, and academic institutions. But one of the insights I have gained from this study has been the recognition that, as individual teachers, we have the power to undermine and even control these forces. I have shown that self-awareness must be a key ingredient of writing teachers' reading behaviors; that given awareness of gender influences and the time to deal with them, teachers can overcome the negative effects of gender biases on assessment of their own students' work. And I have explained the importance of sharing the perspectives of feminist theorists, such as Cixous and Kennard, who acknowledge strong male-female behavioral similarities and renounce the binary oppositions so prevalent in most feminist theory today. A methodology that includes attention to process can give rise to maternal teaching patterns (such as nurturing self-reliance, encouraging dialogue, and providing opportunities for active participation in learning), which are employed by both male and female writing teachers. In this way, our classrooms can become more equitable environments.

I have also shown that as important a force as gender is, and as much as we should recognize its influence, we need to keep in mind its place within a whole range of factors, such as race and class, which affect the ways in which we interact with our students. Especially given the increasingly multicultural context of our classrooms, trying to study gender in isolation is not a useful activity. In fact, concentrating just on gender could prove *harmful* in that it might keep us from understanding the full context of our students' experiences. The complexities of our existence as gendered beings are so entwined with racial, cultural, economic, moral, and even psychological realities that we would be wise to acknowledge that they, too, are significant issues.

For me, though, perhaps most important has been the realization that as an academic community, we must be more assertive about defining ourselves in terms of our teaching, not in terms of theory derived from other spheres. Throughout this text I have examined the connections between reader-response theory, feminist theory, and the rhetorical situation of teachers reading student texts. However, although the majority of theoretical evidence suggests strong associations, my studies show that the reading differences that theorists find when males and females read literature do not necessarily occur when teachers read and react to student writing. Thus, as teachers, we do not merely convert theory into practice; rather our practice is one of the *sources* of theory as well as its main validation. As part of the ongoing dialogue that seeks to define and shape the field of composition, our classroom practices can speak to us in ways that theory can never perceive. Understanding this is central to our growth as a profession.

Appendixes
Notes
Works Cited

Appendix A
Reader-Response Theorists:
A Brief Discussion

The following reader-response theorists, although not central to studies of gender and reading, interpret the act of reading in such a way as to make gender an implicit key ingredient in the reading-teaching experience. Their ideas provoke many questions about the gendered dynamics of teachers reading student texts.

Georges Poulet

Poulet (1980) discusses reading as a transforming experience. As we read, the text ceases to be an object and becomes a part of our inner consciousness. We, in turn, give up a part of this consciousness to become a part of the consciousness that has created the text. The words, images, and ideas that have existed only as marks on the page take on a new existence in our minds, dependent now upon our consciousness rather than the author's. For a time, we tacitly agree to "think the thoughts of another," allowing another "I" to replace our own. Reading, for Poulet, is a merging, an act of will on the author's part—an act of acquiescence on the reader's part.

One question we need to examine, then, is how Poulet's theory applies to us as readers when we evaluate student texts. In our judgmental roles, do we join with the text as completely as he suggests? Or do we hold back so much of ourselves that we are not able to make a total commitment? As teachers, is it possible for us to temporarily share minds with the student author or to so totally efface ourselves that we, in effect, disappear? Poulet speaks of a point at which the author and the reader converge, a point at which the reader is able to bring alive the ideas formulated by the author. "This process," says Iser of Poulet, "is dependent on two conditions: the life story of the author must be shut out of the work and the individual disposition of the reader must be shut out of the act of reading . . . an adequate basis for the author-reader relationship . . . can only come about through the negation of the author's own life-story and the reader's own disposition" (66). Poulet, of course, is talking about the reading of fiction. But his ideas seem antithetical to the whole circumstance of a freshman composition class, where the sum of the papers is often the author's life story and where the teacher-critic brings to bear his or her own experience in reading the student's piece. Many times, especially in conference, the author and the reader sit face-to-face; neither can be negated or even momentarily set aside.

As teachers, this inability to erase the author places us in a double bind. When we read a student text, not only do we not submerge ourselves in the text, we make a conscious effort not to. The evaluation part of our job asks us to live up to the myth of the objective, distanced reader. We must not let our own pasts or personalities either enter or control. Yet as people, we cannot deny what we bring to the text or repress the fact that we bring anything at all. We are the sum total of our training and experience, and we must use all of that to be effective judges of our students and their work.

Wolfgang Iser

Iser, too, sees the act of reading as a transactive experience, and he recognizes the importance of looking at the actions involved in responding to the text. Just as his fellow reader-response critics, he examines the reader of literature. We have to ask, though, if the kinds of responses he notes are valid in teacher-student essay situations or if a different kind of reading comes into play. If Iser's readers, like Poulet's, suspend their conscious selves, merging with the "I" of the text, does the same hold true when the text is no longer fiction, or do we use our minds differently when we read nonfiction prose? Student essays usually have no element of escapism as does fiction. If illusion building is, as Iser suggests, a key strategy authors use to draw us into the text, what happens to the reader when illusion building is no longer part of the author's capability or goal?

Iser discusses a need for a consistent meaning "we can incorporate in our own imaginative world." "Reading," he explains, "reflects the structure of experience to the extent that we must suspend the ideas and attitudes that shape our own personality before we can experience the unfamiliar world of the literary text" (65). But when we read student papers, do we sometimes find this incorporation impossible because, as males or females, we are excluded by certain topics or forms? Maleness-femaleness may be so strong an aspect of our personalities that it cannot be suspended. If male topics, for example (if there are such things), are so alien to the female that she can never match her perception of reality to the reality of the textual world, she might be missing a step as she critically reads.

Iser reasons that the reader creates his or her own experience and that this creation "must include relations comparable to those which the original producer underwent . . . with the perceiver, as with the artist, there must be an ordering of the elements in the whole that is in form . . . the same as the process of organization the creator of the work consciously experienced" (62). Fine for literature. We can live vicariously through skillfully wrought texts. But when we read student papers, we are responding to pieces in which the creator often did *not* consciously experience a coherent process of organization or in which the creator often *did* have a coherent process in mind but did not succeed in re-creating it on the page. As readers, we may often be "confronted by narrative techniques that establish links between things we find difficult to connect" (63), such as the one Wayne Booth labels "unreliable narrator." But Iser is speaking about conscious authorial choices and decisions. When we read student papers, the confusion or confounding of our expectations is often not an intentional ploy on the author's part but a result of poor or undeveloped skills. Sometimes we almost seem to be interpreting student texts in spite of the author rather than at his invitation, and the transactive nature of reading that Iser and Poulet see is radically changed. In effect, we are not only prevented from reliving the experience, we are often at great pains to understand it, even on a surface level. Surely as we seek ways to move past our first subjective (and often unconscious) responses toward a more helpful reading of student essays, we recognize the pitfalls inherent in lean ability: the students are in the midst of a learning-to-write process, and weaknesses are certain to occur. However, the influence of gender on our interpretations suggests the usefulness of a more inner-directed awareness of our own reading process as we wrestle with our students' texts.

Stanley Fish

For Fish, the key question when reading is not What does the text mean? but What does the text do? He warns against denying any human, subjective response and eschews the idea of one "correct" reading of a text. The text is a fluid event that changes according to the reader. Like Iser, he discusses the strategies accomplished authors use to bring the different possibilities of the text into play. As we have already noticed, though, when we read student papers, the author's experience—and intent—is often not reflected directly or coherently in his or her language and, therefore, is not part of the student's meaning. The meaning still resides in the author's mind. What seems like strategy may be the result of lack of skill or control. What we are trying to interpret in a freshman paper, then, is questionable. The text often does not "do" what the author meant, and as readers, we are unable to function effectively. If Fish is correct that conscious in-depth reading cannot occur without the text working on our feelings, we need to know to what extent masculinity-femininity colors what we perceive. How much of the text caters to our gender identities, and how much of the text displeases us because of the same? What happens, too, to Fish's notion of "interpretive communities" when we examine it in the context of a freshman writing class? Those of us who have ever tried to agree on a paper's grade are aware of the myriad difficulties that arise in selecting criteria and of the subjectivity that inevitably intrudes. The basis for our grades may lie in our past experience (which differs from person to person), in our training (which alters from teacher to teacher, from department to department, from school to school), or in our personalities (which change according to multiple components, of which gender is most certainly key).

Louise Rosenblatt

Rosenblatt (1978) depicts an evenly balanced reading event, placing equal emphasis upon text and reader. The text, she writes, "must be thought of as an event in time. It is not an object or an ideal entity. It happens during a coming-together, a compenetration, of a reader and a text. The reader brings to the text his past experience and his present personality. Under the magnetism of the ordered symbols of the text [rises] . . . a new experience, which he sees as the poem" (12). Her writing has strong bearing on this discussion in two important ways. First, because we bring the sum of who we are to each reading of each text and because gender is a key ingredient of that sum, we need to realize how our gender operates when we respond to student writing. The teacher and the student must both assume responsibility for the learning experience, but as teachers, we have an obligation to guide that experience effectively. Full awareness of all the variables involved and of how they function can help us respond more successfully.

It is when Rosenblatt describes the kinds of reading we do however that she suggests a second issue we need to investigate. We perform, she contends, two kinds of reading: *aesthetic*, in which "the reader's attention is centered directly on what he is living through during his relationship with that particular text" (25); and *efferent*, in which "the reader's attention is focused primarily on what will remain as the residue *after* the reading—the information to be acquired, the logical solution to a problem, the actions to be carried out" (23).

When we read our students' work, though, something else is happening. We want to be aesthetically pleased; certainly we penalize our students when that does not occur. And we must read efferently, looking for the information that will help us conference our students. But we also read evaluatively, for unfortunately, that is the end result of our educational system. And this evaluative stance places us above and to one side of the writing, causing us to question many of the reader-response theorists in relation to our task. How plausible do Iser and Poulet, Holland and Fish remain if we speak of reading as moving beyond a subjective losing of or searching for one's identity in the text and add an evaluative dimension to the discussion? What does remain strong is the necessity of studying ourselves and our reactions without giving in to the deception that the issue of gender can be absent from our quest, for it is when we discuss our responses and our interactions with our students that the issue of gender heightens.

Appendix B
The Student Essays

The Drinking Age

One of the most controversial issues between young adults and state legislators is the drinking age. The drinking age is a state law that governs when a person is legally able to buy and consume alcohol. In many states such as New Hampshire, Massachusetts, and Maine, the minimum age to legally purchase and drink liquor is 20. This law, however, is ignored by many 18 and 19 year old people because they are treated as adults in every respect with the exception of drinking alcohol. Drinking requires responsibility and decision making, yet many more responsibilities are placed on 18 and 19 year olds. Therefore, I feel the drinking age should be lowered to 18 years old.

People begin to take total responsibilities for their future when they turn 18 and decisions that could affect the rest of their life must be made. For example, when I turned 18, I was faced with the conflict of working for my dad or going to college. I finally decided to go to college because I wanted to become a chemical engineer. But with that decision, I was immediately confronted with the question of what college would provide me the best college experience I am able to afford. After much thought, I finally chose the University of New Hampshire. Now, currently enrolled at U.N.H., I have to meet the obligation of getting the most out of my college education. I feel that this task will demand much more responsibility and thought than drinking will ever require.

A person 18 years old also becomes totally responsible for all his actions and is punished as an adult in the United States judicial system. For example, if the police arrested me for first degree murder, I would be given a court date and tried for my offense. If the verdict was guilty, I would be sent to jail with all the other violent criminals. The court would not consider lightening my sentence because I am a responsible, legal adult. It seems only right that if an 18 year old can be sent to jail, then he should be given the right to drink alcohol.

Legislators have passed a law saying that anyone serving liquor in restaurants must be at least 18 years old. They are also discussing a law that will place total liability on the server if someone gets drunk. Why then are law makers willing to let young adults serve large quantities of alcohol and be accountable for the customers' actions, but deny them the right to consume it themselves? The only obvious answer is that legislators must feel that 18 year olds have enough responsibility to make decisions for someone else, but not for themselves. In my opinion, these two laws contradict the purpose of the drinking age, which is to keep those below the legal age away from alcohol.

Another responsibility that 18 year olds encounter is voting. Voting has been part of the American way of life since the appointment of the first president and involves much more than just punching a hole into a card. It requires objective thinking, rational decision making, and obligation. For example, when I vote for the president, I don't make a decision until after I have analyzed what each candidate has to offer. I will eventually choose the person who I believe the country will benefit the most from. But while I am voting, I am also contributing to the existence of a democracy. It is a duty that every U.S. citizen should participate in. When establishing the voting age, Congress must have felt certain that 18 is the age when people are capable of making rational decisions and will fulfill the necessary obligation to the democratic process. I find it hard to accept that Congress regards 18 year olds as responsible adults and state legislators don't.

Perhaps the most demanding responsibility placed on 18 year olds is the draft registration. The purpose of the registration is to obtain an accurate list of those people who are old enough to go to war. When a person turns 18, he must register for the draft. The draft is a system devised by the federal government to obtain military forces if war becomes evident. The system involves pulling birth dates out of a barrel. The first birth date chosen will determine the first group of people to go to war. The second date pulled will be the second group to go, and so on up until all 365 days have been chosen. In short, if my birthday was chosen first, I would have to drop my college education, my job, and essentially my life, because I have a commitment to fight for my country. War is ugly and the chances of dying are very good. Millions of people, including myself, hope it will never begin. If war does start, however, I will be expected to fight and, if necessary, die for my country, because I am 18 years old and old enough to cope with the obligation of handing my life over to the United States government. Legislators are wrong if they feel that drinking requires more responsibility and maturity than fighting in a war does.

The legal age to drink liquor in many states is 20 years old. I feel this law should be lowered to 18 because 18 year olds are required to be responsible for things much more demanding than drinking. It is unfair to force some-one who is 18 to die for his country but prohibit him from consuming liquor. It is only right to change all the laws that treat 18 year olds as adults to 2), or lower the drinking age to 18.

Euthanasia

Euthanasia, according to Webster, is the "act of painlessly putting to death a person suffering from a terminal and/or incurable disease." It stems from the Greek words "eu" meaning good, and "thanasia," meaning death. More commonly called mercy killing, euthanasia is a practice that can be dated as far back as the ancient Greek civilization. Yet today euthanasia is illegal, and I don't believe it should be. We are granted in this country the right to life. Should we not be granted the right to death as well? I believe the individual should have the right to a peaceful and painless death if he so chooses. Euthanasia should not be considered a crime.

Both passive and active euthanasia are illegal in the United States, but are they really criminal acts? Passive euthanasia entails not putting a person on a life support machine to keep him alive; no drugs or artificial measures are used. Active euthanasia, on the other hand, involves taking an active role in the hastening of the patient's death. It involves pulling the plug of the life support machine, administering drugs, or in some way inducing a patient's death. Americans feel that no one has the right to perform such acts, even if the patient asks for his death. But society is beginning to accept somewhat more liberal views.

Due to the increasing sympathy for many victims, such as Karen Ann Quinlan, some cases have been brought to court where a judge reviews the case, then points the finger. You may die, you must live. What gives them the right to play God? Why does society feel the judge has more of a right to make this life decision than the patient himself, his family, or doctor? Dying is not something that should be decided by a judge. It is a private matter. This decision by a judge is not an example of justice. It's an example of injustice.

The two major arguments to euthanasia are the moral and religious ar-gument. Many feel it is immoral to kill people, especially when a patient can not make the decision for himself due to his sickened state. Morality is concerned with principles of right and wrong conduct. How can society and judges decide for these patients and their families what is right? It is not immoral to release these suffering victims from further torment; it is im-moral not to. It is more immoral to step in and take control of these people's

lives when they ask you not to. Today's technically advanced society can
keep patients that would otherwise be declared biologically dead, alive.
The brain may be dead, but these machines can eat, breathe, and live for
these patients, so that they can "live" for years. I feel our society must
reassess its thinking, beliefs, and morals, to keep up with modern times.

The religious argument can best be summed up by the words of my
neighbor; "God gives life. God alone has the right to take it away." This is
true, but when that existence can no longer be called life, or when that gift
of life has turned into a curse, the man must take over. The quality of that
life must be taken into consideration.

Euthanasia is not indiscriminate killing, and it does not propose to make
legal the active killing of the mentally retarded or the other so called bur-
dens of society. It concerns those who can not be rehabilitated, and those
who wish to give up the right to life so that they may end their suffering
because no cure is possible.Imagine yourself sixty or seventy years from
now, suffering from an incurable or painful disease. Providing Medicare still
exists, it is inadequate to cover your medical expenses. You live your final
months, or years, in agony and continual pain. The disease slowly consumes
your whole body. The medicine helps relieve the pain somewhat, but
mostly it just prolongs the process and the suffering. It is not inhumane to
let these elderly peacefully rest, to allow someone with no hope of recovery,
and who asks to, to be allowed to end their suffering and to be allowed to
die. We feel compassion enough for our suffering pets to put them out of
their misery, but not other humans.

We are dealing with humans, with people. I spoke with a nurse from the
children's ward at Boston City Hospital. She said, "I think it's especially
hard when dealing with children. They are just poor little victims. You see
them suffering and you have to feel for them. I think it's even harder on the
parents, who can do nothing to help. It is just a matter of time. The parents
pray to God to help, to stop the pain, then they turn to the doctors. They
took an oath to stop suffering and save lives. They help sometimes, although
they can't admit it."

What if you were the parent of a child that was in an accident that destroyed his brain or paralyzed him? He is placed on a life support machine
because he can no longer take care of his own biological functions. You visit
him every day, yet he does not, he can not recognize you. You watch him
regress to a small shrunken figure. Imagine the anguish you'd feel being
totally helpless. As a parent, wouldn't you like to be able to make a decision,
to help stop the needless suffering?

For this reason, many people write living wills, addressed to their family,
doctor, and lawyer, that state if the time comes when they can no longer
make decisions for their own future, there will be a testament of his wishes.
It is not legally binding, but it does place a certain moral obligation on the

persons addressed. It asks that if there is no reasonable expectation of recovery from some physical or mental mishap that they be allowed to die, and not be kept alive by artificial means. These people don't fear death as much as they fear the indignity of helplessness, deterioration, and hopeless pain. Like it or not, we are all going to die, and it may not be in our sleep or at a time convenient for us. Euthanasia is a reality and it is one we as individuals and as a society must give consideration to. It is not a form of murder. Murder is the infringement upon someone's right to life. Euthanasia is the voluntary giving up of that right. Should that be considered a crime?

Tough Guys

Well girls, the days of chivalry, knights in shining armor, respect, and roses have ended. That's right. We've drifted into a new era: the age of tough guys "who think they can do as they please." This line from a popular tune suitably sums up the situation, and you don't need to look far to find numerous examples of these gorgeous romping, stomping female satisfying men. After all, they *are* everything a girl could ever want, right? Wrong.

The truth is these dime a dozen showboats are probably the biggest jokes to hit town, and are becoming more numerous by the minute. With their bulging biceps, manly chests, and melting eyes, these gods are sought after night and day. The great mystery is what keeps these fellows in commission. They must be doing something right. The lengths some girls will go to in order to meet one of them is enough to make me want to throw up. All you have to do is simply take a look at the weekend activities on campus.

The definitive choice of where to go and what to do on Friday and Saturday nights always seems to end up being the ever popular Frat parties and Ladies Teas. These events are carefully planned out by the sly little devils to "catch a girl." For reasons unknown to me, these circus events are frequented by many a female, and you can always count on packed and crowded quarters at the lucky Frat that evening. Just push your way through the door, stick out your little hand for the door guard to mark, and move on in. Once your eyes have become accustomed to the dim lights and smoky air, you can fight your way to the bar for that free beer you came for. And if you're really lucky, by the time you get there your arms and legs will still be intact and only three beers will be penetrating your chic new sweater. Now you can settle in and either partake in the competition or sit back and observe these tough guys in action. After having been to one too many of these gala events, I've decided that the only pleasure I derive from them is choosing the latter of the two.

These fast talking studs will never cease to amaze me. They actually seem to derive pleasure out of using and abusing members of the opposite sex. In one hour or less, they can convince females of their innocent intentions and sincere ways. They move in slowly but steadily. It starts with a comfortable chair, very casual, nothing too serious. Then they pour the lucky girl a beer or two and stealthily slip an agile arm about her shoulders, while pretending to listen intently to her conversation. Then it's off to the dance floor: a few fast dances, a few more beers, and maybe a waltz. Now on to the dark corner to make out for a while and consume one last beer. At this point, if all goes according to plans, the handsome young "gentleman" will escort the rather intoxicated young lady up the stairs to one of the ready and waiting bedrooms. And bingo. Another one bites the dust. But the worst is yet to come: rejection and the realization of having played the fool.

The lies and one liners spouted off effortlessly by the majority of the male species are by no means any consolation to an unfortunate female. Lines like "I really enjoyed being with you and hope that we can continue our relationship" are for the birds. Another all time favorite, "Sure, I'll be in touch. I'll call you soon," only serves to raise hopes sky high just to let them come crashing down even harder. The victim finally realizes after countless hours of waiting by the phone that she has been used, lied to, and cast aside to take another number. So the saga continues, these meat market events go on, and females are continually subjected to the abuses of the male ego. Girls put up with getting gawked at and poked at by the less courteous, tricked and abused by the many experts in the field of deception. All of this in the hopes of finding that one special relationship. Is it really worth it? For some of us, all of this has been pushed just a bit too far.

I, for one, am not turned on by the growing number of handsome gents who reveal charm and a tough body while momentarily concealing a brain the size of a pea and a personality no bigger than an acorn. Sure, these tough guys can feign affection momentarily, but a closer look will reveal their true personalities. After all, their charming fronts can only last for so long. They're out to get a girl in the sack, and many are no longer even ashamed to let people know it. They seem to wear their reputations like a crown as they strut around campus, expecting everyone to bow down and worship them. Not all girls are satisfied with getting drunk and laid by a gorgeous hunk with no sense of responsibility, no feelings, and no respect for himself or for others. I often wonder whether these fellows have ever had a meaningful relationship with anyone, or if they've ever tried to genuinely appreciate company other than their own. I hope that someday they learn to pride themselves in more than conquering females and creating meaningless relationships.

Don't get me wrong—I'm not saying that *all* males are unreliable slugs; I'm sure there are a few out there somewhere who have managed to retain a bit of respect and sincerity. Nor am I suggesting that all Frat brothers are of this type (although those that aren't seem few and far between) or that only in Frats can you find these heavenly specimens. I'm sure I could learn to put up with and even like some of the gorgeous Greek gods had I met them under different circumstances. And no matter where you look, you can always count on running into the truly tough guys. They're everywhere, and you can just bet they're waiting to pounce on their next prey. I'm also not oblivious to the fact that it takes two to tango. I realize some girls are also out for what they can get and do ask for it. But nevertheless, the bare facts remain.

Tough guys who seem to think they can do as they please are overshadowing and outnumbering the nice guys. They're discouraging girls from seeking out or accepting what could be an enjoyable friendship or a loving relationship. When time after time any genuine spark of affection is met with a sneer and any expressed wish to continue a relationship is cast aside, a girl is bound to abandon faith and take on a cold attitude merely for protection. This isn't my idea of a fun time. Nor is getting burned, losing trust, or watching my girlfriends go through the treadmill because of some jerk who just won't pay them the time of day after building their hopes up sky high.

So here's one lady who will be sticking to the smaller events with true friends and sincere company as opposed to the commotion and abuse experienced in the midst of total strangers and studly men. Hopefully, this way I will be spared the agony of encountering too many of these all too common casanovas, and will find a trace of the respect and honesty that seems to have vanished in today's new age of the tough guys.

How to Be a Hit with the Girls

I know what you're thinking. You've been at the university for three months and you still haven't found a girlfriend. You've tried everything from dying your hair red to wearing exotic colognes, but still nothing seems to work. Well don't worry because I'm going to show you how to meet the girl of your dreams and carry on a meaningful relationship. At least for one night.

The first thing you must know is how to meet that special someone. The key to this is knowing where to look. The favorite spot of most U.N.H. students is still Nick's. Not only is this a good place to find women, but also if the impossible does happen and you do strike out, there is plenty of alcohol available so that you can forget about your misfortune.

But don't worry about striking out. If you do everything right, everything will go as planned. First of all, you must enter the building very slowly. This will give the women a chance to check you out and see how macho you are. Then head for the bar. At the bar you can check out the girls while having a drink. Of course you will have to know what to look for in a girl.

Studies show that the average man prefers a girl who is about 5'7" and blonde. She must also have a good personality, both from the front and the back.

After finding a girl of your dreams, just relax and finish your drink. It is important not to rush into things as you may do things that make you look silly. An example of this would be spilling your drink all over your prospective mate because you were in too much of a rush to notice the waiter who was on a collision course with you. Just sit back and enjoy your drink.

Once you have finished that drink, take a deep breath and, with your best John Wayne imitation, sidle up to her table. At this point, after lowering your voice two octaves, ask her if you can buy her a drink. Because of a combination of your natural charisma and the fact that the amount of cologne you are wearing is making her dizzy, she will, without a doubt, ask you to sit down. After sitting down, have a few drinks and then ask her to dance.

After an enjoyable night full of drinking and dancing, offer to walk your little Miss America home. Remember though, once you get there, don't be too pushy. Just give her a friendly kiss and ask her if you can take her to dinner sometime. By this time she will be putty in your hands and, without a doubt, will say yes.

And then, before you know it, it will be time to get ready for that big date. You must be sure to do everything exactly right in preparation for that big date or you may never see your dreamgirl again. Oh, the pressure!

The first of your problems is how to dress. This, however, is not a particularly difficult one to solve. Your main objective in dressing is to blow your date away with your great taste in clothing. This can be done quite simply starting with a black pair of Haggar stretch slacks and a red silk Gucci shirt, unbuttoned half-way down to show anything that might be growing on your chest. Next, get a pair of shoes with an unpronounceable Italian name. Driving gloves are optional, but if you do use them, make sure that they don't clash with your rented Ferrari.

Of course, during the ride to the restaurant you must remember to be a perfect gentleman, keeping at least one hand on the wheel. It would also be a good idea to keep at least 50% of your clothing on. Pre-dinner petting, in excess, tends to diminish one's appetite and focus attention on activities other than eating. Remember to concentrate on the road and not your date's physique.

Hopefully you will get to the restaurant in one piece. And when you do you must again know how to act properly. Be sure to help her take her jacket off and hold her chair for her. Also, contrary to popular belief, it is not a good idea to order in French. This is especially true if you are eating at an Italian restaurant. And remember to keep the conversation light. Discussing Darwin's Theory of Physio-psychological evolution tends to drag down the evening. Basically, just be natural and don't drink too much as you will need your wits about you later on.

After an evening of good food and stimulating conversation, invite your date back to your place for a drink. At this point, extreme caution must be taken in order to promote the proper atmosphere. First, after entering your apartment, invite her to sit on the bear skin rug in front of a roaring fire. Don't forget to make sure that you have a fireplace before lighting a roaring fire. If you don't, you will have to make do with a candle. Next, bring in a bottle of white wine. Don't forget to remind her that wine goes bad in about 15 minutes and that the two of you should finish the gallon bottle long before this period of time arrives. Then, turn on a Johnny Mathis record, put your arm around her, and start drinking.

Once you have finished the bottle of wine and listened to the complete works of Johnny Mathis, it's time to make your move. All you have to do is tell her she is more beautiful than a flower in spring and kiss her. Then invite her into your bedroom to see your red satin sheets and mirrored ceiling. Then, once you are in the bedroom, turn on your cassette tape of Ravel's Bolero and offer to show her what making love is all about. If you have paid attention to my advice, all you will need is a cigarette for afterwards. Remember, it's not how you play the game that counts, but rather it's how much you enjoy yourself while playing.

Appendix C
The Oral Responses

Phillips points out that as interviewers, when we allow our respondents to express their feelings without fear of disapproval, we often receive an almost embarrassing richness of information, which increases further the more we remain nondirective and minimize our own influence. In short, people like to talk about themselves, and given an interested listener, they will do so at length. In the written responses, the teachers primarily attended to the task at hand, commenting only on the papers they were grading. In the interviews, however, this changed dramatically.

Even though I did not ask, each instructor at some point brought up gender-related differences among the students. In fact, throughout all of the interviews, the teachers spoke quite freely about sexual stereotyping and their gender perceptions of their students, issues they had not raised in their written responses. Given the opportunity to vocalize their feelings, the teachers candidly revealed gender-based biases. I suspect this key difference between the written and oral responses was due not only to the interview situation but because most people would hesitate to put in writing many of the frank and often controversial opinions about students that arose. The oral responses indicate the following gender-related patterns.

Teachers of both sexes said they expect certain writing behaviors from females and certain writing behaviors from males, and they are often surprised—and displeased—when students deviate from imaginary gender norms. The instructors note key differences in topic selection, approach or strategy, and language choice. Table C.1 lists the differences teachers reported seeing between their male and female students.

The instructors reported seeing clear distinctions between the topics male and female students choose. For example, everyone identified the writer of "The Drinking Age" as a male, even though I had not attached a

Table C.1. Teachers' Reported Perceptions of Male and Female Writing Behaviors

Males	Females
Choose topics they can talk about objectively	Choose more personal topics
Role play to cover their actual feelings	Give more personal and more emotional responses
Make more assertions	Ask more questions
Use satire often	Explore subjects more seriously
See only end results	Are more concerned with process
Avoid personal narratives	Are drawn toward personal narratives
Use "male" words	Would not use "male" words
Use the generic "he"	Use feminine pronouns

student name. One male instructor explained, "For me at least, three to one, male students choose this topic over female students. It's a terrible cliche topic. Male students focus on it more than female students do." A female instructor disclosed, "This may be my own prejudice or bias, but I think young men tend to be more concerned with topics like these. This concern about laws, about what's right and what's wrong. . . . A man tends to let the law determine behavior. A woman tends to question the reason behind something." Conversely, everyone "knew" the writer of the euthanasia paper was a woman because, as one male claimed, "women are more willing to approach a subject like death or aging and people's problems with death and aging more directly sympathetically than men."

Teachers often identified approach or strategy as a direct indication of gender. Note the differences they claimed to notice between masculine and feminine ploys. First, remarks about male students by both male and female instructors:

There'll be a bit more role playing with male students, or a little bit more ways of covering themselves as a writer so they won't be embarrassed.

Male students have a tendency to cover, to turn what seems to be based on personal anxiety or uncertainties or bad experience into a kind of, well, on the one hand aggressive and on the other hand sort of playful posture, a semi-humorous stance that finally completely dissociates the writer from any genuine responsibility for what he's saying.

I have found that it's much easier for a young man to speak with authority. Men are more comfortable, and it seems so much easier making really didactic statements: this is the way it is. And the drinking age paper makes all kinds of assumptions. It shows real confidence. I just assume a male wrote it.

Men are more concerned with the *act* of writing, the end results of writing. What have we got here? Either we've got a good theme or a bad theme. I think the stereotyped version of men is not how to get there, but the end results.

Men struggle more with personal narrative because they're more autonomous. Making connections is very difficult for them.

"Responsibility" and "decision making" are words or phrases that freshman males tend to use. In the drinking age paper, the words "murder," "jail," "criminal," "court" . . . males use these words.

Males always use the generic "he."

Both male and female teachers, however, reported seeing their women students' strategies in a different light:

Women have a different approach than men. They have more personal, emotional responses to a problem.

Women have so much more at stake and so much less power. They tend to be far more threatened. Sometimes, though, women's writing is more honest. There's really no holding back.

I think a woman wrote the paper on euthanasia. Just the way the writer used rhetorical questions. It seems somehow to make less assumptions. Women just seem less likely to go right out and make a statement. They'll say it in a question.

For me, women seem more concerned with the process of getting there, and that makes their writing seem more honest than men's.

Women . . . girls . . . well it has to do with their psychological development. They have tended to take relationships between people much more seriously and have tended to see themselves in some kind of web of relationships while they're growing up. As young adults they value connection enormously, and most narratives are about our relationships with other people.

Women, especially freshmen, wouldn't use words like those in the drinking age paper in freshman English . . . maybe when they're older . . . in legal briefs.

Women use feminine pronouns.

These teachers seemed to have definite images or expectations about what their students, as males and females, do. Perhaps as they read the four student essays, they began to form preliminary judgments about the work based on how well the elements in the text matched their expectations of appropriate gender behaviors. Culler's suggestion that we interpret the same texts differently according to our presuppositions, as well as according to the context of the reading situation, illuminates many of the teachers' oral responses. As I mentioned earlier, these revealing comments could be due in large part to the opportunity I gave the teachers to talk without censure on my part and to the provocative papers I introduced. But something more complex is happening here that moves beyond the mere chance to speak freely. The "How to Be a Hit with the Girls" essay in particular illustrates how topic influences that are strong enough may indeed affect assessment. Significant, though, is that even here the pull of the evaluative context is so powerful that males and females react in similar ways. Rather than pushing each gender in opposite directions, these gender influences unify teachers' perspectives, aligning both sexes so closely that no significant gender differences appear.

Appendix D
Peter and Joanne: Student Papers

Benefits of Breast Feeding

After researching breast milk and breast feeding, and having breastfed for 18 months, I have reached a conclusion. It is this. Formula, unless under prescription, should be illegal and mothers who opt to bottle feed, after knowing the facts, ought to be illegal as well. Is this a strong statement? This is only because you haven't read and witnessed what I have. I will do my best in my much too short five pages to win you over to somewhere in the vicinity of my opinion. Let's start off with some startling facts.

Breast fed babies have little or no ear infections. In fact here is a long list of some of the fewer illnesses: There is less diarrhea, (less constipation as well) and "other gastrointestinal disorders." There is less respiratory infections and less rashes. It has been shown that extended breast feeding may help prevent asthma and eczema! Breast fed babies are less apt to obtain bronchitis, pneumonia, botulism, hyperthyroidism, polio, influenza, and may help protect against rubella.

An element in breast milk helps the baby start reproducing his own antibodies. This is really neat. Approximately eighty percent of the cells in breast milk are microphages. These cells kill fungi, bacteria and viruses. And would you believe that these cells help to stop the growth of cancer cells, and could reduce risk of multiple sclerosis?

A mother's milk is designed for her own baby. Certain nutrients are in the breasts at different times. There is a "built in time table" which accompanies the baby during each stage of growth and development. Breast milk is always changing, whereas formula is the same old junk day in and day out.

I used to watch a T.V. show that often had some comments on breast milk. Once a fact was stated that breast feeding helps reduce many allergies later on in life. If you are allergic to chocolate, strawberries, milk, wheat, and pollen, quite possibly your mother may take the blame because she did not breast feed you. Of course, she did not know at the time. Today's mothers do, so what is their excuse? Some are embarrassed about it; they don't want to hurt their figures; they don't want to be tied down. Such loathsome responses for not wanting to give what's best for your baby. I have no patience for such women, especially if they can't claim ignorance to what I know.

Breast milk is so convenient. I loved being able to go on outings, such as fishing trips or camping, without having to worry about whether I had enough formula or if it would spoil. My "bottles" were already there, and the milk was as fresh as it gets!

What joy I got out of producing my own child's milk! I would look at my healthy plump son and think "I did that. I provided all of his nutrition. He is thriving so because of my milk." What a maternal feeling this gave me, and how my baby benefits from my sureness!

One cannot match the intimacy or bonding a woman gets from breast-feeding her baby. A woman once told me this: "One can get the same satisfaction from holding a child on the lap and reading it a story or feeding it on your lap." I told her this: "It is obvious you have never breast fed." A bottle feeding mother can only come close to having the intimacy and bonding a breast feeding mother has with her baby.

A breast feeding mom tends to want to feed her baby more because of such facts as painful engorgement. This is when the breasts become too full of milk. Breast feeding is also very enjoyable for mom and baby. I loved taking every few hours, five to ten minutes, and laying down with my baby, just he and I and my very nutritious milk.

I am pregnant again with my second child. I will breast feed again. I couldn't possibly give my baby imitation milk. I want the very best for my baby.

My first baby would not touch the raunchy stuff called formula. If the second one is as smart as the first, he won't touch it either.

Untitled (Economics)

I think that the entire world should abolish the production of all currency, both paper and coin. In the United States, for example, stop printing green pieces of paper worth amounts of dollars along with copper and silver colored, round pieces of metallic alloys worth fractional amounts of dollars. Rather than using material pieces of paper to designate money, we should just use the number which really tells how much, how many, or how few dollars we have. Rather than carrying cash, checks, and credit cards, we would just have a card similar to an ATM card that would have the number of monetary units we had in our possession. We could even retain the name dollar if we so desired for these units. To help clarify the point I am trying to make, take, for example, the amount of money two hundred forty seven dollars and twenty-eight cents, or $247.28 in the shorter form. It is not important at all that we call the monetary amount dollars and cents or that we use symbols for the names. What is important is that there is the number 247.28. It is the number of dollars and cents, in this case 247.28 of them, that tell us how much worth is in something, how much we have in our possession, or how much we can or cannot spend.

The benefits of adopting this idea far outweigh the costs. First of all, this stopping of material currency production would actually save the federal government money. To substantiate this, one must consider the historical fact that in the early sixties the U.S. Department of the Treasury stopped making pennies entirely out of copper and silver coins entirely out of silver, adding zinc, magnesium, and aluminum to form less expensive alloys. The bottom line was that it was actually costing more to produce the coins than they were actually worth. Thus saving money when making it is an essential idea for the federal government. Just think how much money would be saved if it no longer had to be produced at all. It couldn't be anywhere nearly as costly to construct and to maintain a network of computers. The Treasury Department would no longer have to bother itself with the duties of printing new and destroying old currencies. Instead, it could focus its efforts on managing this gigantic system.

Banking and financial services would benefit from the adoption of such an idea because their efforts could focus entirely upon loans; they would no longer need tellers to disperse cash sums because there would be no more cash. We would all benefit from this because we would no longer need to stand in a long line awaiting the next available teller to service our needs. Take for example, check cashing; rather than receiving a paycheck each week an employee would receive credit to his account for the amount of monetary units earned during the week. As part of producing a weekly payroll, the employer could provide the service of making that credit to the employees' accounts. Thus, the only time anyone would need a bank would be when they wanted to get a loan and appointments could be made to conduct such business. Thus, there would no longer be those long lines at the banks that snake around the front of the tellers, resembling the lines at the rides in Disneyland. ATM-like machines could easily be used for repayment of loans; and if a loan was delinquent, the creditor could attach a warning of sorts on the account so that anytime an amount of monetary units was added to that account the lien that the creditor held would become evident. Thus, payment could be made through an automatic transfer of an appropriate number of monetary units. Thus, a bank would never lose out on a loan due to nonpayment.

Another benefit to the banks and financial services would come as a result of the no longer needed credit cards and check books that would be replaced by the solitary card that would have that useful account number on it. Items bought on credit could be paid for in similar fashion as a loan would be repaid, and there would be no need at all for writing checks. Incidentally, checks could only further make the idea that much more appealing as they have subtracted from the importance of having cash on hand. Checks are simple pieces of paper, but they are most importantly numbers. Custom made dollar bills perhaps, but it is the numbers that make them so.

Perhaps the biggest benefit to be gained from implementing this idea would be that crime would decrease substantially. It would be impossible for kidnappers and terrorists to demand ransom for their hostages because they would not want monetary units transferred to their accounts, because then their identities would be revealed. Illegal purchases of drugs would become next to nonexistent because of the difficulty involved in doctoring such transactions to make them appear legal. How many items could someone sell to the same person repeatedly for the same price? I don't think it would be too late before suspicions arose. Prostitutes would be faced with a similar dilemma in trying to accept payment from their customers. Muggers would be limited to taking their victims' watches, chains, clothes, and the like. They would not be able to steal anyone's monetary unit card because they would need to know how to access that card without the cardholder's account number. As aforementioned credit cards and checks would no longer be used and therefore could not be stolen. Travelers' checks would also not be necessary once the entire world adopted this plan and thus they too would not be the subject of thievery. All anyone would need if they left home would be that solitary monetary unit card.

Worldwide adoption of this plan is essential for it to work effectively. There is no reason why it could not be adopted because despite the fact that there are dollars, pounds, yen, pesos, and rubles, they are all represented by numbers. The only difference between a dollar and a peso is the spelling. They are both nouns used as adjectives when thought of in the sense of this plan to revolutionize money. The real difference between the two is that the peso is only worth something like one two-thousandth of a dollar. Thus all that would be needed to transform dollars to pesos would be a very simple formula of multiplying by 2000. As exchange rates change, the formula changes, and it can be used reciprocally to determine the exchange of dollars for pesos. In this case by multiplying by a two-thousandth.

In closing, it must be noted that the ultimate benefit in adopting this plan would be the power and ability of the global network of computers to monitor the transactions with pinpoint accuracy. Accounting would then be easy to complete through utilization of the computers, and they could be checked through frequent printouts. Thus, all the out of work bank tellers, drug dealers, and prostitutes could go to work at the various accounting offices that would be essential to make the system work for all of us. The world would truly be a much better place if paper and coin currency were abolished.

Drag Racing

"Someday you'll learn about cars; in fact, you'll be the crew chief for a world famous drag racer." If anyone had told me that five years ago I would have laughed hysterically. I was the one who couldn't find the dipstick to check the oil in my own car. I didn't even know how to pump my own gas. Then I married an auto maniac and, suddenly, it was either sit in the garage while my husband, Jeff, tinkered on his latest hot rod, or sit in the house alone. I opted for the garage and decided that if I was going to be out there then I might as well learn something.

The first knowledge I acquired on my journey to becoming an automotive assistant is that there is no way to work on a car engine and remain clean. I used to be such a neat person—not anymore! In fact, I now have as many grease stained jeans as Jeff. I learned to tolerate the grease. I even read in one of his racing magazines, National Dragster, that engine grease is very good for your skin; it keeps it supple. So, women of the world, find a car and use that grease! Soon you too will notice a definite improvement in your skin tone. People may question the aroma, but they will love the softness.

Besides getting dirty, I have learned other things working beside Jeff in the garage. I can finally say that I know where the dipstick is located on almost any make of car. At the gas station, I can use the self-service pump. I know what a cam looks like, where pistons are located, how to change the spark plugs, what a timing light is used for, and a multitude of other mechanical trivia.

Once, while Jeff was taking a motor apart, he challenged me by saying, "I bet you can't do this." That's all it took. I was off. (He had an old motor tucked away in a corner of the garage.) As I would remove a part, Jeff would explain what it was. A piston, rocker arms, push rods, lifters, oil pump, crank shaft, and on and on. Three hours later, I sat surrounded by hundreds of engine parts. He then attempted to continue the challenge by saying, "I bet you can't put it all back together." I glanced down at the mountain of oil drenched parts and defiantly said, "No way!" I had proven myself with the first challenge and I sure wasn't foolish enough to fall for that trick twice in the same day. Besides, my battered knuckles couldn't have survived another round with the tight spaces of the motor.

In the past five years, Jeff has owned three different hot rods. (A term used by auto addicts.) His first was a shiny black 1923 Ford Model T, affectionately known as a "T" bucket. It was a two-seater and everything that wasn't black was chrome. To watch it travel down the road was dazzling and I got to do a lot of watching. Being able to transport only two passengers at a time, most trips we made involved one of the kids riding with Jeff (they took turns) and me tagging along behind in my beat up old Pontiac with the other two kids. It didn't hurt my feelings when Jeff decided to sell the "bucket" in order to build another street rod.

The next car was gorgeous! A 1934 Ford three window coupe. You could fit five people in this beauty, so my days of bringing up the rear were finally over. It was painted a handsome two-tone brown and instead of having a trunk it sported a nifty pop out seat, called a rumbleseat. All three of the kids fit back in there as though it was designed especially with them in mind. It had black matted running boards below the driver and passenger doors and whenever we were riding, I could visualize Bonnie and Clyde going off to pull another bank job. It was a car like this that they were driving when they were gunned down. Jeff kept this gem of a car for two years when he decided it was time to get back into drag racing.

The race car turned out to be a 1967 Chevrolet Camaro. He painted this the same shiny black as the "T" bucket, but this one had a name! Across each side of the car, in 12" high, flaming hot pink letters, it read "Movin Violations." While the previous cars were built for show, the Camaro was built strictly for racing. Just for you car buffs out there, it is powered by a potent L88 427 engine with a high performance racing cam. The transmission is automatic, controlled by a B&M shift kit and the 29" slicks (racing tires) are mounted on polished Centerline wheels. In case you are not a car person and all of this sounds like a foreign language, then let me explain by putting it in terms we can all understand. Everything involved with racing is EXPENSIVE. The motor alone is worth $5000, the transmission has eaten $800, another $1000 has gone into the wheels and tires. The cam was a bargain at $329 and there is easily another $6000 that has been poured into "miscellaneous" parts. The body of the car was actually one of the cheaper items. Jeff found it hidden in the bushes of a house in Barrington and offered the owner $1000. The owner was only too glad to get it off his property. If, by chance, you are looking for a way to put a strain on your budget, then by all means build a race car.

Jeff races this expensive play toy at New England Dragway in Epping, New Hampshire. Drag racing bears no resemblance to its sister sport of stock car racing where you go round and round an oval track. Drag racing is a straight shot down a quarter mile, two lane track. The object is to start at a set of staging lights, called a Christmas tree (similar to a set of traffic lights). Seventy-five feet before reaching the lights, the driver will stop his car, the track crew will spray a generous amount of water on the ground, and the driver will lock his front brakes and depress the gas pedal to the floor. This causes him to sit there and spin his tires, creating a cloud of smoke, and heating the rubber of his slicks. All this is to provide better traction for the race. This area of the track is called the "bleach box" because until racers found out that water would do the trick they sprayed bleach on the ground. After leaving the "bleach box," two drivers move up to the Christmas tree; when the lights turn green, they must accelerate as quickly as possible. In order to win, you must beat your opponent to the finish line. If not, you are done racing for the day. If you are the winner, you move on to the next round, until finally, only two drivers remain to pair off. A day at the races can be over after one run (approximately ten seconds) or it can last into the night.

When Jeff decided to get back into racing, he had raced back in the 70's before I knew him, he was trying to make me feel like I was part of it. He said, "Hon, every driver has a crew chief and I can't think of anyone I'd rather have for the job. So, what do you say, will you take it?" I was flabbergasted, honored beyond words, so choked up with emotion that I could barely reply, "What's a crew chief?" Jeff patiently explained that a crew chief has many responsibilities, but as I look back on the conversation, I recall that he was very vague as to the specifics of my newly bestowed title. Since then I have come to learn that in my case, most times, being a crew chief means running for burgers, drinks, or other non-automotive essentials. My only race related duty consists of recording the air temperature and speed he runs each race, and making note of the size of the jets he is using in the carburetors. (Jets are tiny brass nozzles that allow gas to flow through the carburetor.) I'm not sure what Jeff does with all of this faithfully compiled information, but he assures me that it is crucial.

While Jeff is racing, I sit in the bleachers and wait anxiously for him to come up to the starting line. My stomach is jumping with butterflies and I try not to think of him getting hurt. Drag racing is a relatively safe sport, but there have been occasions when drivers have been injured and even killed. Once I saw a car roll over and burst into flames. The driver crawled out of the tangled wreck and walked away. The safety features that are mandatory on race cars are a necessary drain on the pocketbooks of all drivers. It doesn't upset me to see Jeff spend $125 on a fireproof jacket. Because the race itself lasts a mere ten seconds you really don't get a chance to spend a lot of time thinking of the danger.

So far Jeff's drag racing career has not brought us any wealth or fame. We rarely make it through a day at the track without something breaking after the first round. The few times that nothing broke he was eliminated during the first round. After being beaten (or the car dying) Jeff returns to the pits, where drivers park and work on their cars, and loads the car onto the trailer. We always stay awhile after he is through to watch and cheer the other drivers we have become friends with. There is a tremendous amount of camaraderie in drag racing. Drivers depend on each other to borrow tools and parts and to lend a helping hand. The other women at the track are friendly and easy to get along with, their common bond being racing itself.

Almost every evening during the week you can find Jeff in the garage repairing and replacing parts on the Camaro so that it will be ready for the following weekend. He calls this the "ironing out the bugs" stage, but I think the "bugs" more closely resemble dinosaurs. I'm sure that someday (soon, I hope) he will reach the point when he is satisfied with the way the car is running and perhaps even begin to win. Winning doesn't seem to be the number one priority of these weekend racers. They ache for the thrill involved with the sport.

In my dreams I often see Jeff on Wide World of Sports, racing side by side with world reknowned racers. There's "Big Daddy" Don Garlits, Don "The Snake" Prudhomme, Kenny "The Budweiser King" Berstien, and right there with them is my husband Jeff "The Speed Demon" Gordon. Then, and only then, I will at long last be able to say, "I'm the crew chief for a world famous drag racer!"

Notes

1. Gender and Reading: Theoretical Indications

1. Like Bleich, Elizabeth A. Flynn (1986) shows that measurable differences exist between the responses of females and the responses of males to works of fiction and poetry. Flynn details a project in which men and women were asked to respond to three short stories. Males, she found, "sometimes react to disturbing stories by rejecting them or dominating them, a strategy . . . women do not often employ. . . . Women more often arrive at meaningful interpretations of stories because they more frequently break free of the submissive entanglement in a text and evaluate characters and events with critical detachment" (285). Women, however, are better able to achieve "a balance between detachment and involvement" (285) and interact on a more personal level with the text. In short, women are more perceptive readers than men. Flynn's article is disturbing because she suggests the existence of an ideal "balanced" reader that in actuality can never exist, but she does point out contrasts between male and female responses, empowering further the premise that gender-based reading differences might occur when teachers read student texts.
2. Personal conversation, 20 September 1989.
3. Linda Peterson also probes the teacher's role. In a discussion of gender and topic choice, she warns us against possible gender preferential treatment: "We need to be conscious that assigning only personal essays in a writing course may give a grade advantage to some students, even if we cannot identify the specific reasons for this advantage and even if we formulate our assignments to encourage the capacities and experiences of both genders . . . perhaps teachers should check all grades for correlations with gender. It is worth knowing if assignments or evaluation procedures privilege the skills, capacities, or experiences of one gender more than another" (6). Moving even closer to our own central

question, Peterson admits how, as a woman, she senses problems when she reads male-oriented texts, and her uneasiness spills over into her process of assessment. She worries candidly that "our evaluation of personal essays should not privilege one mode of conceiving the self over another. This is easier said than done. Young male writers commonly choose to recount a confrontation with nature: a challenging hike up a mountain, an experience with parachuting, a canoe trip down a white water river with a couple of buddies and a case of beer. As a woman, I am not unfamiliar with experiences in nature, but they tend to be contemplative rather than confrontational. The conventional male form of experience . . . seems puerile to me" (10–11). Peterson notices that she is unable to make strong connections with her male students' essays. Holland would say she is not able to find in the text any patterns that mirror her own identity. "Examining our own gender-linked preferences," Peterson warns, "may be necessary before we assign and evaluate students' writing" (11).

4. When Kolodny (1985) refers to reading as a process of sorting out the "structures of signification" in any text, she involves us in semiotics, or the science of signs. This field lies beyond the scope of this study, but I want to mention a key point made by Terry Eagleton (1983), in which he explains that "whatever we perceive in the text is perceived only by contrast and difference: an element which had no differential relation to any other would remain invisible. . . . The literary work, indeed, is a continual generating and violating of expectations, a complex interplay of the regular and the random, norms and deviations, routinized patterns and dramatic familiarizations" (102–3). As we read student papers, then, we constantly (and probably unconsciously) measure the writing against our own personal, professional, and cultural experience as well as against other student papers we have seen. We need to be able to recognize the "signs" in the text that trigger our responses; we need to be aware of the clues in the text that signal differences and likenesses to what we have previously experienced.

Judith Fetterley (1978) also discusses how women have been excluded as participating readers from male-centered texts, especially in American literature. She demonstrates how female readers of American fiction are forced to identify as males and engage in experiences foreign to their self-knowledge. She urges a feminist critic "to become a resisting rather than an assenting reader and, by this refusal to assent, to begin the process of exorcising the male mind that has been implanted in us" (xxii).

5. Though the French theorists would feel comfortable, for the most part, with sections of the models offered by Kolodny, Schweikart, and Kennard, their own distrust of what they see as the West's methodical sup-

pression of female experience gives their writing a more pointedly antimale edge. Their ideological framework rests on the immediately obvious physical differences between men and women, with women's physiology and sexuality the prime vehicles of feminine expression. Conscious expression of sexual pleasure—*jouissance*—helps women restructure the phallogocentric concepts so effectively silencing the female perspective. Without this bodily statement, Julia Kristeva (1981) sees little hope for women to make themselves heard in a male-discourse-centered community. In contrasting women's sexuality with male discourse conventions, she insists that to rupture those conventions and express themselves fully, women must challenge existing patriarchal systems.

Two additional writers, Luce Irigiray and Monique Wittig, help flesh out this theoretical background. Wittig aligns most closely perhaps with Kennard when she urges women to understand their differences from each other as well as their differences from men. Like Kennard, she would have us learn of women by exploring the multiplicity of women's sexual and social characteristics rather than defining them solely in opposition to men. Irigiray, too, asks women to make visible what society has veiled: their explicitly sexual physical and libidinal differences from men. She maintains, as A. R. Jones (1985) points out, that if men are responsible for "the reigning binary system of meaning—identity/ other, man/nature, reason/chaos, man/woman—women, relegated to the negative and passive pole of this hierarchy, are not implicated in the creation of its myths . . . to the extent that the female body is seen as a direct source of female writing, a powerful alternative discourse seems possible: to write from the body is to re-create the world" (366).

These writers offer feminine models of writing—of *ecriture feminine*—that invite women to inscribe in every possible way their bodily urges—or *pulsions*—on the text, bringing blood and fluid, physical expressions of oral and anal drives together in a freeing social discourse, and they translate this to a similar sexual interpretation of reading that is hardly new. (Stephen Marcus [1987] notes that in a letter to Ethel Smyth, Virginia Woolf admits, "Sometimes I think heaven must be one continuous unexhausted reading. It is a disembodied trance-like intense rapture that used to seize me as a girl, and comes back now and again down here, with a violence that lays me low . . . the state of reading consists in the complete elimination of the *ego*; and it's the ego that erects itself like another part of the body I don't dare to name" [86]). But except for an oddly fuzzy interpretation of reading as a sort of emotional and intellectual masturbation over the printed page, these perspectives offer us little in the way of a concrete model of reading that we can translate for our own use.

2. Gender Patterns: Reading Student Texts

1. See Georges Poulet, "Criticism and the Experience of Interiority," *Reader-Response Criticism*, ed. Jane P. Tompkins (Baltimore: Johns Hopkins U, 1980) 41–49.
2. Wolfgang Iser, "The Reading Process: A Phenomenological Approach," *Reader-Response Criticism*, ed. Jane P. Tompkins (1980) 65.

3. Gender and Writing Teachers: The Maternal Paradigm

1. Other useful sources of advice for successful nondirective interviews can be found in H. H. Hyman et al. (1954); C. A. Moser and G. Kalton (1971); John Lofland (1971); and R. L. Gorden (1975). Particularly helpful, too, for suggesting ways to gain maximum data are those ethnographic interviewing techniques described by Michael H. Agar (1980); D. Hymes (1978); James P. Spradley (1979); Shirley Brice Heath (1983); Martyn Hammerty and Paul Atkinson (1983); and John L. Wengle (1988).
2. Mishler is not alone in valuing contextual research. Kenneth Gergen (1978) writes: "In the attempt to isolate a given stimulus from the complex in which it is normally embedded, its meaning within the normative cultural framework is often obscured or destroyed. When subjects are exposed to an event out of its normal context they may be forced into reactions that are unique to the situation and have little or no relationship to their behavior in the normal setting" (510).

   We also find support for contextually grounded research in cognitive psychology; see especially John D. Bransford (1979) and Lev S. Vygotsky (1979), both of whom emphasize the importance of observing people in their normal learning situations.

4. Gender and Teaching Writing: Conclusions, Implications, and Guidelines

1. For another excellent discussion of the troublesome breech between theory and practice, see Peter Elbow's *What is English?*, 86–87.
2. Studies of professional writers echo these differences. Although I am concerned here with student writers, texts such as Abel's *Writing and Sexual Difference* are important because they analyze the ways in which women writers grapple with a system of primarily male conventions and because they discuss how women translate these conventions into literary differences of structure, genre, voice, and plot. Many of the questions the essays in this text raise, such as How is female iden-

tity and/or experience reflected in female writing? or Is there such a thing as a female aesthetic?, would be useful questions to ask in terms of our student writers as well.

Although some work at the college level has been conducted that examines the effects of gender on teacher-student interaction (see especially Kajander 1976; Richardson, Cook, and Macke 1981), little has been done with the specific context of teachers and students in a college conference-based writing course. Yet this particular teacher-student relationship is such a close one, we need to obtain much more information.

Works Cited

Abel, Elizabeth, ed. *Writing and Sexual Difference*. Chicago: U of Chicago P, 1982.

Agar, Michael H. *The Professional Stranger*. New York: Academic, 1980.

Ardener, Edwin. "Belief and the Problem of Women." *Perceiving Women*. Ed. Shirley Ardener. N.p.: Malaby, 1975. 1–28.

Ardener, Shirley. *Defining Females*. New York: Wiley, 1978.

Belenky, Mary Field, B. M. Clinchy, N. R. Goldberger, and J. M. Tarule. *Women's Ways of Knowing*. New York: Basic, 1986.

Bellugi, Ursula, and Roger Brown. "Three Processes in the Child's Acquisition of Syntax." *Journal of Verbal Learning and Verbal Behavior* 5 (1966): 325–27.

Benstock, Shari, ed. *Feminist Issues in Literary Scholarship*. Bloomington: Indiana UP, 1987.

Berelson, Bernard. *Content Analysis in Communication Research*. Glencoe, IL: Free, 1952.

Bleich, David. "Gender Interests in Reading and Language." Flynn and Schweikart. 234–66.

Booth, Wayne. *The Rhetoric of Fiction*. Chicago: U of Chicago P, 1961.

Bransford, John D. *Human Cognition*. Belmont, CA: Wadsworth, 1979.

Brenner, Michael, Jennifer Brown, and David Cantor, eds. *The Research Interview*. London: Academic, 1985.

Brown, Jennifer, and Jonathan Sime. "A Methodology for Accounts." *Social Method and Social Life*. Ed. Michael Brenner. New York: Academic, 1981.

Calkins, Lucy McCormick. "Forming Research Communities among Naturalistic Researchers." *Perspectives on Research and Scholarship in Com-*

position. Ed. Ben W. McClelland and Timothy Donovan. New York: MLA, 1985. 125–44.

Cambridge, Barbara L. "Equal Opportunity Writing Classrooms: Accommodating Interactional Differences Between Genders in the Classroom." Unpublished ms. 1987.

Cannell, Charles F., and Robert L. Kahn. "The Collection of Data by Interviewing." *Research Methods in the Behavioral Sciences.* Ed. Leon Festinger and Daniel Katz. New York: Dryden, 1953.

Carroll, Joyce Armstrong. "Process into Product: Teacher Awareness of the Writing Process Affects Students' Written Products." *New Directions in Composition Research.* Ed. Richard Beach and Lillian S. Bridwell. New York: Guilford, 1984.

Chodorow, Nancy J. "Gender, Relation, and Difference in Psychoanalytic Perspective." *The Future of Difference* Ed. H. Eisenstein and A. Jardine. New Brunswick: Rutgers UP, 1987. 3–19.

———. *The Reproduction of Mothering.* Berkeley: U of California P, 1978.

Cixous, Hélène. "An Exchange with Hélène Cixous." Conley. 129–61.

Conley, Verona A. *Hélène Cixous: Writing the Feminine.* Lincoln, NE: U of Nebraska P, 1984.

Constantinople, Anne. "Masculinity-Femininity: An Exception to the Famous Dictum?" *Psychological Bulletin* 80 (1973): 389–407.

Crawford, Mary, and Roger Chaffin. "The Reader's Construction of Meaning: Cognitive Research on Gender and Comprehension." Flynn and Schweikart. 3–30.

Crowley, Sharon. *A Teacher's Guide to Deconstruction.* Champaign, IL: NCTE, 1989.

Culler, Jonathan. "Literary Competence." Tompkins. 101–17.

———. *On Deconstruction.* Ithaca: Cornell UP, 1982.

Dean, John P., Robert L. Eichhorn, and Lois R. Dean. "Observation and Interviewing." *An Introduction to Social Research.* Ed. John T. Doby. 2nd ed. New York: Appleton, 1967.

D'Eloia, Sarah. Letter to Thomas Farrell. 1 Dec. 1976. "The Female and Male Modes of Rhetoric." *College English* 40.8 (1979): 909–21.

Denzin, Norman K. *Sociological Methods: A Sourcebook.* 2nd ed. New York: McGraw, 1978.

Dinnerstein, Dorothy. "Higamous-Hogamous." *Ways of Reading.* Ed. David Bartholomae and Anthony Petrosky. New York: St. Martin's, 1967. 168–201.

Eagleton, Terry. *Literary Theory*. Minneapolis: U of Minnesota P, 1983.

Eisenstein, Hester, and A. Jardine, eds. *The Future of Difference*. New Brunswick: Rutgers UP, 1987.

Elbow, Peter. *What is English*. New York: MLA, 1990.

Elbow, Peter, and Pat Belanoff. "Portfolios as a Substitute for Proficiency Exams." *College Composition and Communication* 37 (Oct. 1986): 336–39.

Emig, Janet. *The Composing Process of Twelfth Graders*. Urbana, IL: NCTE, 1971.

——. *The Web of Meaning: Essays on Writing, Teaching, Learning, and Thinking*. Ed. Dixie Goswami and Maureen Butler. Upper Montclair, NJ: Boynton, 1983.

Faigley, Lester. "Competing Theories of Process: A Critique and a Proposal." *College English* 48.6 (1986): 527–42.

Farrell, Thomas J. "The Female and Male Modes of Rhetoric." *College English* 40.8 (1979): 909–21.

Fetterley, Judith. *The Resisting Reader*. Bloomington: Indiana UP, 1978.

Fish, Stanley E. "Interpreting the Variorum." Tompkins 164–84.

——. *Is There a Text in This Class?* Cambridge, MA: Harvard UP, 1980.

——. "Literature in the Reader: Affective Stylistics." Tompkins. 70–100.

Flynn, Elizabeth A. "Gender and Reading." Flynn and Schweikart. 267–88.

Flynn, Elizabeth A., and Patrocinio P. Schweikart, eds. *Gender and Reading*. Baltimore: Johns Hopkins UP, 1986.

Freire, Paulo. *The Pedagogy of the Oppressed*. New York: Continuum, 1968.

Gannett, Cinthia. "Gender and Journals: Life and Text in College Composition." Diss. U of New Hampshire, 1987.

Gardiner, Judith Kegan. "On Female Identity and Writing by Women." *Critical Inquiry* 8 (1981): 347–61.

Garrison, Roger. *One-to-One: Making Writing Instruction Effective*. New York: Harper, 1981.

Gergen, Kenneth. "Experimentation in Social Psychology: A Reappraisal." *European Journal of Social Psychology* 8 (1978): 507–27.

Gilligan, Carol. *In a Different Voice*. Cambridge, MA: Harvard UP, 1982.

Goldberg, Herb. *The Hazards of Being Male*. 10th anniversary ed. New York: Signet, 1987.

Good, Thomas L., and Jere Brophy. *Looking in Classrooms*. Cambridge, MA: Harper, 1987.

Gorden, R. L. *Interviewing: Strategy, Techniques, and Tactics*. Homewood, IL: Dorsey, 1975.

Graves, Donald. "A New Look at Writing Research." *Perspectives on Writing in Grades 1–8*. Ed. Shirley Haley-James. Champaign, IL: NCTE, 1981. 93–117.

———. *A Researcher Learns to Write*. Exeter, NH: Heinemann, 1984.

———. "Sex Differences in Children's Writing." *Elementary English* 50 (Oct. 1973): 1101–6.

Hammerty, Martyn, and Paul Atkinson. *Ethnography: Principles in Practice*. New York: Tavistock, 1983.

Heath, Shirley Brice. *Ways with Words*. Cambridge: Cambridge UP, 1983.

Heilbrun, Alfred B. *Human Sex Role Behavior*. New York: Regamon, 1981.

Holland, Norman N. "Unity Identity Text Self." Tompkins. 118–33.

Hyman, H. H. et al. *Interviewing in Social Research*. Chicago: U of Chicago P, 1954.

Hymes, D. *What is Ethnography?* Sociolinguistic Paper 45. Austin: Southwest Educ. Dev. Lab, 1978.

Irigiray, Luce. "And the One Doesn't Stir Without the Other." *Signs* 7 (Fall 1981): 60–67.

Irmscher, William. *Teaching Expository Writing*. New York: Holt, 1979.

Iser, Wolfgang. "The Reading Process: A Phenomenological Approach." Tompkins. 50–69.

Jones, A. R. "Writing the Body: Toward an Understanding of *l'Ecriture feminine*." *Feminist Criticism*. Ed. Elaine Showalter. New York: Pantheon, 1985. 361–77.

Kajander, Cheryl A. "The Effects of Instructor and Student Sex on Verbal Behaviors in College Classrooms." Diss. U of Texas at Austin, 1976.

Kennard, Jean E. "Ourself Behind Ourself: A Theory for Lesbian Readers." Flynn and Schweikart. 63–80.

Keroes, Jo. "Different Voices: Gender and the Content of Student Writing." Unpublished ms. San Francisco, 1987.

Kinneavy, James L., and C. Robert Kline, Jr. "Composition and Related Fields." *Teaching Composition: 10 Bibliographic Essays*. Ed. Gary Tate. Fort Worth: Texas Christian UP, 1976.

Kolodny, Annette. "Dancing Through the Minefield: Some Observations on the Theory, Practice, and Politics of a Feminist Literary Criticism."

Feminist Criticism. Ed. Elaine Showalter. New York: Pantheon, 1985. 144–67.

———. "Turning the Lens on 'The Panther Captivity': A Feminist Exercise in Practical Criticism." Abel. 159–75.

Kristeva, Julia. "Oscillations Between Power and Denial." *New French Feminisms*. Ed. Elaine Marks and Isabelle de Courtivron. New York: Schocken, 1981. 165–67.

Leinhardt, G., A. M. Seewald, and M. Engel. "Learning What's Taught: Sex Differences in Instruction." *Journal of Educational Psychology* 71 (1979): 432–39.

Lofland, John. *Analyzing Social Settings*. Belmont, CA: Wadsworth, 1971.

McConnell-Ginet, Sally. "Difference and Language: A Linguist's Perspective." Eisenstein and Jardine. 157–66.

Marcus, Stephen. *Freud and the Culture of Psychoanalysis: Studies in the Transition from Victorian Humanism to Modernity*. New York: Norton, 1987.

Merton, Robert K., M. Fiske, and P. Kendall. *The Focused Interview*. Glencoe, IL: Free, 1956.

Miller, Susan. *Rescuing the Subject*. Carbondale: Southern Illinois UP, 1989.

———. *Textual Carnivals*. Carbondale: Southern Illinois UP, 1991.

Mills, Charles Wright. *The Sociological Imagination*. New York: Oxford UP, 1959.

Mishler, Elliot G. "Meaning in Context: Is There Any Other Kind?" *Harvard Educational Review* 49 (1979): 1–19.

———. *Research Interviewing, Context and Narrative*. Cambridge, MA: Harvard UP, 1986.

Moser, C. A., and G. Kalton. *Survey Methods in Social Investigation*. London: Heineman, 1971.

Muehl, D., ed. *A Manual for Coders*. Ann Arbor: Inst. for Social Research, 1961.

Murray, Donald M. *A Writer Teaches Writing*. Boston: Houghton, 1968.

Newkirk, Thomas. "How Students Read Student Papers." *Written Communication* 1 (July 1984): 283–305.

North, Stephen M. *The Making of Knowledge in Composition: Portrait of an Emerging Field*. Upper Montclair, NJ: Boynton, 1987.

Ong, Walter J., S.J. "The Writer's Audience is Always a Fiction." *PMLA* 90 (Jan. 1975): 9–21.

Perrin, Noel. "The Androgynous Man." *The Dolphin Reader*. Ed. Douglas Hunt. Boston: Houghton, 1987. 208–11.

Peterson, Linda. "Gender and Autobiographical Writing: The Implications for Teaching." Unpublished ms. 1987.

Phillips, Bernard. *Social Research: Strategy and Tactics*. New York: Macmillan, 1966.

Piggott, Margaret B. "Sexist Roadblocks in Inventing, Focusing, and Writing." *College English* 40.8 (1979): 922–27.

Poulet, Georges. "Criticism and the Experience of Interiority." Tompkins. 41–49.

Richards, I. A. *Practical Criticism*. New York: Harcourt, 1929.

Richardson, I., J. Cook, and A. Macke. "Classroom Management Strategies of Male and Female University Professors." *Issues in Sex, Gender, and Society*. Ed. L. Richardson and V. Taylor. Lexington, MA: Heath, 1981.

Rosenblatt, Louise. *Literature as Exploration*. New York: Noble, 1976.

———. *The Reader, the Text, the Poem*. Carbondale: Southern Illinois UP, 1978.

Ruddick, Sarah. "Maternal Thinking." *Feminist Studies* 6 (1980): 70–96.

Schatzman, Leonard, and A. Strauss. *Field Research*. Englewood Cliffs, NJ: Prentice, 1973.

Scholes, Robert. *Textual Power*. New Haven: Yale UP, 1985.

Schweikart, Patrocinio P. "Reading Ourselves: Toward a Feminist Theory of Reading." Flynn and Schweikart. 31–62.

Sherrill, Anne. "Does Sex Make a Difference? Sex Roles and Territorial Expansion in the Narratives of Seventh Graders, Tenth Graders and College Freshmen." Unpublished ms. 1979.

Showalter, Elaine. *Speaking of Gender*. New York: Routledge, 1989.

Sommers, Nancy. "Revision in the Composing Process: A Case Study of College Freshmen and Experienced Adult Writers." Diss. Boston U, 1979.

Spear, Karen. *Sharing Writing: Peer Response Groups in English Classes*. Portsmouth, NH: Boynton, 1988.

Spradley, James P. *The Ethnographic Interview*. New York: Holt, 1979.

Squire, James. *The Responses of Adolescents While Reading Four Short Stories*. Champaign, IL: NCTE, 1964.

Stallard, C. "An Analysis of the Writing Behavior of Good Student Writers." *Research in the Teaching of English* 8 (Summer 1974): 206–18.

Tinberg, Howard B. "'An Enlargement of Observation': More on Theory

Building in the Composition Classroom." *College Composition and Communication* 42 (Feb. 1991): 36–44.

Tompkins, Jane P., ed. *Reader-Response Criticism*. Baltimore: Johns Hopkins UP, 1980.

Vygotsky, Lev S. *Thought and Language*. Cambridge, MA: MIT, 1979.

Weiler, Kathleen. *Women Teaching for Change*. New York: Bergin, 1988.

Weiss, Neal. *Introductory Statistics*. Reading, MA: Addison, 1982.

Wengle, John L. *Ethnographers in the Field*. Tuscaloosa: U of Alabama P, 1988.

White, Janet. "Gender Differences and the Place and Status of Literacy in the School Curriculum." Unpublished ms. San Francisco, 1984.

Wimsatt, W. K. *The Verbal Icon*. Kentucky: U of Kentucky P, 1954.

Wittig, Monique. *Les Guerilleres*. New York: Viking, 1971.

Zinker, Joseph. *Creative Process in Gestalt Therapy*. New York: Random, 1977.

Donnalee Rubin directs the Center for Writing Across the Curriculum at Salem State College in Massachusetts, where she teaches courses in writing, composition theory, and contemporary pedagogical approaches. A graduate of the doctoral program in English at the University of New Hampshire, her current research interests include collaborative learning, the relationship between writing and cognitive development, and the connections between literary criticism and composition theory.